T0114232

Pope Benedict XVI

JOURNEY TO ST. PETER OF THE FIELDS

Through Randolph/Rootstown Townships

A Historical Sketch

Robert F. Winkler

Order this book online at www.trafford.com
or email orders@trafford.com

Most Trafford titles are also available at major online book retailers.

© Copyright 2011 Robert F. Winkler.
All rights reserved. No part of this publication may be reproduced, stored in a retrieval
system, or transmitted, in any form or by any means, electronic, mechanical, photocopying,
recording, or otherwise, without the written prior permission of the author.

Printed in the United States of America.

ISBN: 978-1-4251-8058-4 (sc)

Trafford rev. 03/07/2011

 www.trafford.com

North America & international
toll-free: 1 888 232 4444 (USA & Canada)
phone: 250 383 6864 ♦ fax: 812 355 4082

Table of Contents

Introduction

This book is dedicated to those parishioners who were instrumental in the development of Randolph and Rootstown Townships in Ohio, where the Catholics of St. Peter's, Rootstown, and the Catholics of St. Joseph's, Randolph, settled as they migrated from Western Europe. Most came from France and Germany.

Chapter I gives a brief history of the development of Randolph and Rootstown Townships. The growth of these two townships is very important and sets the stage for the development of the two Catholic churches described in the following chapters. Finally *Journey to St. Peter of the Fields* would most probably never have occurred if not for Randolph's and Rootstown's early residents.

Many of the early settlers of Rootstown and nearby New Milford were not of the Roman Catholic faith as the settlers of the southwestern part of Portage County near Randolph were. Major credit is due them, however, for their great pioneer and religious work in that area of Rootstown. This book documents the journey from early 1800's to present day.

Today, of course, hundreds of Catholics and Protestant families live side by side in both of these areas.

The accuracy of specific times, dates, and places of events was sometimes difficult, yet of primary concern for this author because many historians and writers do not agree on these time lines. The works cited, however, and the dozens of interviews conducted by this writer have provided the information as written. The book eventually centers on the 1868 parish of St. Peter of the Fields, Rootstown.

St. Joseph's, Randolph, is included because that church was established in 1831 as a mission church of St. John's, Canton, Ohio. St. Peter's then followed as a mission church of St. Joseph's. The new church was the determination of certain St. Joseph parishioners from the Rootstown area who wanted their own church in Rootstown; their determination led to its establishment.

It is the author's hope that the appeal of this book resides in the strength and power of the oral histories and first person stories contained herein, but also in the development of the two townships and the two churches.

May this history and these early pioneers inspire those of us now living here to live our lives in the imitation of Christ.

Chapters I through X contain many photos which the author hopes will help explain the total story of this book. Additionally, Chapter XI contains documents, charts, letters, reports and other photographs of special interest.

There are many more photographs and reports of various church activities occurring throughout the years at St. Peters, too numerous to include here. They can be found, however, in the archives of the historic church of St. Peter of the Fields.

On May 28, 2010 Bishop George V. Murry S.J. Bishop of the Youngstown Diocese announced a reconfiguration plan for the Diocese. The plan called for certain parishes to eventually be closed, others to merge & still others to become collaborative parishes.

St. Peter of the Fields, Rootstown & St. Joseph, Randolph would collaborate meaning they would share one or more priests, retain separate identities, but share resources, staff & programming, thus leaving these two historic parishes in tact.

This collaboration is currently in progress at the writing of this book.

Chapter I

Growth of Selected
Randolph and Rootstown Townships

The two land masses now known as Randolph and Rootstown Townships lay within the area of Ohio referred to as the Western Reserve. The Western Reserve, comprising approximately 3.5 million acres, was originally granted to Connecticut in 1662 by Charles II, King of England. In 1786, Connecticut ceded her claim to land companies for this large land mass running 120 miles west from the Pennsylvania line and 50 miles to the south. See Chapter XI (Document Section, #1) for a map of the Western Reserve.

Moses Cleaveland (spelled with an extra "a") led the original surveying party into the Western Reserve in 1795. The city of Cleveland was named after him. When the surveying was done in 1796, 1798, and 1802 for the townships, the southern part of what was known as Hudson Township was formed into the Township of Franklin made up of Rootstown, Brimfield, Randolph, Suffield, Tallmadge, Portage, Edinburg, and Charleston. When the surveying was done for the various townships, Randolph was numbered "one" of the eighth range. Rootstown was not yet numbered.

This part of the land grant of Randolph Township was drawn by Colonel Lemuel Storrs of Middletown, Connecticut, whose son was Henry Randolph Storrs. The township of Randolph was named after the colonel's son.

Before 1830, there were few Germans or so called "Pennamites" (PA) in the region. By 1836, however, half of the population was referred to as Yankee and the other half as from Pennsylvania, Virginia, or Germany. It is not clear who the Yankees were, but it is suspected they were from eastern parts of the United States.

There were several well known and outstanding leaders in Randolph Township who were instrumental in its development years: Oliver Dickenson (1805-1842), grandfather of Walter Johnson Dickenson, author of *Pioneer History* (1802-1865); Reverend Joseph Merriam (1823-1888),Oliver's pastor; Dr. Joseph Price (1846-1895), who was an old-style family doctor (traveled by horse from home to home); and William Merrill, who operated a successful lath machine factory and other businesses at the center of Randolph.

The Portage County Detective Association was established in 1831, and a Lt. David Elmore was appointed as officer-in-charge for Randolph. Several men from each of the townships served as assistants in their respective areas. The population of the Randolph and Rootstown areas in 1802 was six persons. By 1810, only eight years later, Randolph had 165 residents. The entire county of Portage had 2,995 inhabitants.

By 1830, twenty years later, Randolph had 690 persons, compared to the county population of 18,826, which was fourth highest in the entire state. Ravenna only had 806 persons in this same year. By 1850, Randolph had 1,732 residents, Rootstown had 1,308, and the entire county had 24,419. Randolph was developing much faster than her surrounding townships. See Chapter XI (Chart Section, Chart #1) regarding population comparisons.

In 1833, after scattered meetings at various homes of Randolph pioneers, a 34' x 34' gathering place was constructed. It was referred to as the Red Meeting House and was to be used for various community purposes. It lasted until 1860 when it was torn down and a new meeting house was built just north of the center of town. In 1885, a new and bigger structure was put on the same site. Meetings were also held at times at the old schoolhouse at the center of town and at a schoolhouse southeast of the center. Many of these residents were Methodists or former Baptists.

Services were also held by a Catholic priest, Rev. Matthias Wirts. Between the years of 1838 and 1840, twenty-five children were baptized by Father Wirts. It is interesting to note that for a time two buildings were constructed, one by the French from Alsace-Loraine, France, and one by Germans from the Hessian states of Germany. Both the French and Germans began worshipping together around 1840. More specific information on the assignments of priests will be dealt with in Chapter II.

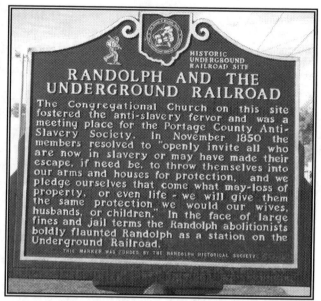

A tragic shooting occurred in Randolph in 1806. A man by the name of John Dever traded a horse for an Indian pony with an old Indian named Nickshaw. Nickshaw felt cheated and sent Indian John Mohawk to kill Dever. Mohawk shot Dan Dever, John's brother, by mistake, blinding him for life.

Another little known, but interesting, piece of history occurred in Randolph in 1818. Eighty prominent Randolph men and women petitioned the Ohio General Assembly to have Ohio secede from the Union because of their opposition to slavery. Among these petitioners were Dr. Joseph Price, Walter Dickersen, and Mr. Merriman, all of whom were well known in Randolph. The Ohio General Assembly accepted the petition, but took no action. In 1861, the southern states seceded from the Union for the opposite reason, thus sowing the seeds of the Civil War.

Several of the prominent Randolph settlers mentioned above were instrumental in setting up an Underground Railroad for slaves moving north prior to and during the Civil War. The plaques pictured here mark the site of that Underground Railroad location and can presently be seen in front of the town hall in Randolph, Ohio.

The history of the many local and county fairs is also very interesting. Several fairs were held in Portage County between 1825 and 1830 by the Sloan family in Ravenna. Other fairs were held in 1842 and 1844, and again in 1879 in Ravenna. Garrettsville also held fairs until 1890 as did Deerfield from 1861 to 1890. Rootstown also held fairs in the 1870s. Palmyra held a horse fair in 1830 and other fairs in the 1880s. In 1890, 20,000 people attended the Portage County Fair in Ravenna. Still, other fairs were held intermittingly in Ravenna until 1929. A fire destroyed most of the Ravenna Fair buildings in 1932. Fairs were again held after WWII in 1946 and 1947 in tents in that city. Randolph also had fairs. The Randolph Fair, founded in 1858, moved to its present location in 1875 on Fairgrounds Road. It is now the only officially recognized Portage County Fair with 85 acres and 64 buildings.

Ephraim Root, a wealthy lawyer from Hartford, Connecticut, and a pioneer of the Connecticut Land Company, came to Rootstown in 1800. He brought Harvey Davinport and a surveyor named Nathaniel Cook. They started to survey the township in the fall of 1800. Mr. Root returned to Connecticut, but came again in the spring of 1801, along with his brother David. They developed an area near what is now Campbellsport, where they built a two-story log house. This structure sat on the four corners of the townships of Ravenna, Charleston, Edinburg and Rootstown. Soon others came from Pennsylvania. By 1804, several families had arrived from Connecticut and settled to the west of Campbellsport near Rootstown. Family names like Caris, Andrews, Chapman, Bostwick, Ellsworth, Bissel, Ward, Roundy, Belding, Coe, Reed, Newbury, Wright, Case, Austin, and Willard became important in the development of the new town called Rootstown and in a settlement a couple miles to the east called New Milford. Rootstown Township was organized and given its name in 1810.

One of the most tragic happenings in early Portage County centered around a man by the name of Nathan Muzzy and his lost love. His disappointment in his love affair with Emma Hale basically ruled his entire life. Nathan, a Revolutionary War soldier, a graduate of Yale and an ordained Congregational minister, left Massachusetts and came first to Marietta, then Portage County where he became a carpenter. In 1801, Nathan Muzzy assisted Ephraim and David Root in building their log house in Rootstown. He had also built a log house for himself in Randolph. Nathan carved his lost love's name (Emma Hale) on an overhead archway to his house and on the outbuildings and trees. He also worked in other areas of the county. In 1812, he built a saw mill for Stephen Mason who was just elected sheriff of the county. Nathan Muzzy died a pauper and a broken man who never got over his lost love of Miss Emma Hale.

The lake that lies west of SR 44 and south of Sandy Lake Road is known as Muzzy Lake, named after Nathan Muzzy. It is this lake and nearby Crystal Lake that were the inducement for the formation of the Rootstown Water Company several years later.

A widely-known character of early Rootstown who was known as Mother Ward lived alone along Crystal Lake, which was "lot eighteen." She could do the work of any man as she was large, muscular, and had great energy. She came from Pennsylvania and made annual trips back home. Her maiden name was Dunfield. Her first husband was killed by Indians. Once she walked from Rootstown to Poland, near the Pennsylvania line, some 40 miles distance.

Several soldiers who served in the Revolutionary War later lived and died in Rootstown. There were at least twelve who served in the War of 1812. Sixty-three served in the Civil War. Eight of these were from the area south of Rootstown, later to be called St. Peter's. Forty-seven soldiers served in World War I, and 163 served in World War II from the township. It is ironic that forty-seven Civil War soldiers are buried in the cemeteries of Rootstown. See Chapter XI (Report Section, Report #1) for the names of those soldiers and others who served later.

In 1800, a Reverend Joseph Badger came from Connecticut and served several Protestant families. A Reverend Giles Cowles also served around 1810. Reverend Joseph Merriam was the first regular or permanent cleric to be assigned. Reverend Henry Shewell was the first pastor of the Methodist Church, 1815.

The first Congregational Church in Rootstown, the oldest church known in the Rootstown area, was established in 1810. A Sunday school for children was established in 1821. The church organ was installed in 1896 as a gift from Mrs. John D. Rockefeller. This organ is still used today, and Mr. Richard Kickline of Alliance, Ohio, continues to maintain it.

The *Pioneer History Book (1802-1865)* refers several times to "the road to the hollow," known as Johnnycake Hollow. In the 1840s, this area was a large industrial park. There were twenty shops and factories located there. Laborers made twenty-five cents per day and skilled workers made forty cents per day. It was reported that eighty persons worked there with a monthly payroll exceeding four thousand dollars. There were fourteen sawmills in the Randolph area at this time. Many of the factories got their power from the creek that flows through the hollow. There were distillers, tanneries, cabinet-shops, other woodworking shops, and a jewelry store which still stands today. It is the third house on the left side south of the bridge on Hartville Road and is now a private home.

In later years, the Keller Brothers Machine Shop and the Randolph Floor Mill became known throughout Ohio. There was talk of Johnnycake becoming the county seat of Portage County. That obviously never happened.

There was little rain between May and October of 1854. On August 8, 1854, according to the *Ravenna Republican* newspaper, a fire started in the engine-room of the grist mill, and many buildings, all wooden, burned. Twenty deaths were reported. The Johnnycake settlement never recovered.

As a result of the Johnnycake tragedy, the population of Randolph began to decline from approximately 1,750 in 1854 to 1,376 in the very early 1900s. In 1930, the population began to grow once again.

By 1850, 7,000 acres of land were under cultivation; corn, oats, wheat, hay, potatoes, and other farm crops were grown. Nearly every farm had a maple sugar camp. Remnants of a sugar camp of long ago can still be found on the Winkler farm on Old Forge Road. Bricks can be dug up throughout the area. In 1850, a number of sea captains (reportedly sixteen), with their families, came from Nantucket and settled in Rootstown.

During the same time period, a company called Reick-McJunkin Co. of Pittsburg purchased milk products from a local factory in Rootstown owned by a Mr. Hudson where the farmers sold their milk. When Mr. Hudson died, the Reick-McJunkin Co. purchased the factory and another large farm on Diagonal Road (now called Cook Road), which is known today as the Harville Farm. Mr. Harville, a well known dairy farmer for many years, passed away at one hundred years of age in the summer of 2008 at Loyalton Nursing Home in Ravenna.

In 1853, Mr. Nelson Converse from Aurora built the first general store in Rootstown. In 1866, the C & P Railroad came to New Milford, a settlement to the east of the center of

Rootstown. It became known as "the station" because that was the only place around with a station. The Depot was large; it had waiting rooms, storerooms, freight houses, and offices. The famously-known station-master was Mr. Lyman Coe. There were a number of train derailments in those early years until the steep grades and curves were graded and fixed. There was also a general store and a grist mill by the tracks. Names like Rood Winans, John Smith, the Scotch family, Jake Kraiss, and Alphonso Hallock were well-known. A Mr. Stein, a sculptor, is believed to have carved the two lions that were in the front yard of the former Hallock residence, just north of the tracks on New Milford Road, also the former residence of Bob Dunn, former Superintendent of Rootstown Schools. These lions have since been moved to Mantua, Ohio.

There were several other businesses like carriage shops, the Horace Camp Cheese Factory (thus Camp Road), and a theater where *Out in the Streets* and *Tony the Convict* were popular plays.

In 1845, an epidemic struck the Rootstown community, and many people died from what was called Black Erysipelas. The only local doctor, Dr. Bassett, was stricken with the disease and died within 48 hours.

Development of the Schools in both Randolph and Rootstown

As stated earlier, the Congregational Church established a Sunday school for children in 1821. In 1804, Mrs. Ephraim Chapman taught two families in the Rootstown area. By 1807, Rootstown had its first small public school. In 1815, a larger school house was built east of the town center; children came from the entire township.

In 1821, a state law was passed authorizing township school districts. In 1844, Randolph established twelve school districts. One such district was established in Rootstown. It was the rule rather than the exception to have all grades in one building with one teacher for all in the early 1800s to 1850s.

In 1832, a Catholic school was established at St. Joseph's, Randolph, by Father John Martin Henni. It is reported to be the oldest Catholic school west of the Alleghenies. That school is still in operation at this writing (2010). Refer to Chapter II for more detailed information on this school.

The public schools, or District Schools as they were originally called, developed into township schools with virtually every township in the county with its own elementary and high school buildings. In later years, for financial reasons, the townships consolidated their schools so that one school served several townships. Examples of those consolidations are as follows: Southeast Schools, which were made up of Palmyra, Paris, Edinburg, Deerfield, and Charlestown, consolidated in 1950; Garfield Schools, which consisted of Freedom, Nelson, and Garrettsville, consolidated in 1951; Ravenna City Schools, which included Ravenna and Ravenna Township, consolidated in 1960; Crestwood Schools, which were made up of Hiram, Mantua, and Shalersville, consolidated in 1964; Waterloo Schools, which consisted of Atwater and Randolph,

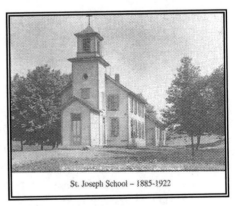

St. Joseph School – 1885-1922

5

consolidated in 1965-1966; and Field Schools, which joined Suffield and Brimfield, consolidated in 1968. Rootstown and Windham schools did not consolidate.

Sources for News in the 19th Century

How did news travel in the early part of the 19th century in Portage County? Obviously news traveled by word of mouth, neighbor to neighbor, at local community gatherings, church meetings, etc., but there were early newspapers as well.

Portage County's long list of newspapers includes the following:

- 1825- *Western Courier* and *Western Public Advertiser*
- 1830- *Ohio Star* in Ravenna which became the *Record Courier* of today, but known earlier as the *Portage County Democrat* and *Portage County Whig*
- 1855- *Hickory Flail* and *Fushion* in Kent
- 1859- *Omnium Gatherum* also known as *The Family Visitor and Literary Casket* in Kent; *Sharp Sickle* in Atwater; *Western Pearl* in Garrettsville; *Whig, Argus, Western Cabinet, Reformer, Canal Advocate, Watchman* and *Western Courier* in Ravenna; *Bugle Echo* in Hiram; *Wide Awake* in Palmyra; *Register, Review and Gazette* in Mantua; *Watchman, Sentinel* and *Plain Dealer* in Ravenna
- 1878- The Democrat and Republican paper became the *Portage County Republican*.
- 1893- The *Graphic* bought out the *Republican*. There was a *Saturday Review* and a *Commercial Bulletin* which became the *Saturday Bulletin* and then the *Kent Bulletin*. Kent also had the *Kent News*.
- 1915- There was the *Kent Tribune* which became the *Ravenna Evening Record* and later the *Record Courier*. The *Kent Tribune* was also connected with the *Ohio Star*.

The Randolph Area, Early 19th Century

The following is a more complete list of early pioneers and businesses in Randolph and Rootstown. Most of these persons came and settled. A few returned to the east. Additionally, a few moved to other areas of the state.

- In 1797, Surveyor Amzi Atwater and assistant Wareham Shepard left after their survey was completed. The first settlers were Bela Hubbard, Salmon Ward, Joseph Harris, Calvin Ward and John Ludington who were from Middleton, Connecticut; Arad Upson came from Plymouth, Connecticut.
- From 1802-03, there were six persons in the township.
- In 1803, Josiah Ward, his wife, and six children came from New York. Jehial Savage and Timothy Culver also arrived during this year. Jehial brought his wife and five children. Aaron Weston, Levi Davis, Carey and Smith (full names unknown) came, but only to trade with Indians and, consequently, did not settle in the area.
- In 1804, Ebenezer Goss came from Plymouth, Connecticut, bringing his wife and four children. Eliakim Merriman moved from Wallingford, Connecticut. Timothy Culver took out a license to keep a tavern, Ebenezer Goss started the first blacksmith shop, and

Eliakim Merriman opened a copper shop all in the same year.

- In 1805, the first mill was built. Hiram Raymond was the first tailor, and Thomas Miller was the first shoe maker. Oliver Dickinson and his family came from East Granville, Massachusetts. Isaac Merriman migrated from Connecticut, and Archibald Coon came from Pennsylvania. Abisha Chapman and John Goss and family arrived from Connecticut. Jeremiah Sabin and son, Abel Sabin, came from Poughkeepsie, New York.

- In 1806, Hiram Raymond, Thomas Miller, Nathan Sears and his son Elisha, and Reverend Henry Ely all came from Connecticut. William Thornton moved from Pennsylvania, and Daniel Cross from Vermont. Nathan Muzzy came from Worcester, Massachusetts. Oliver Dickinson, Bela Hubbard, and Josiah Ward each set out an orchard in 1806.

- In 1808, Calvin Ward and Timothy Culver built the first distillery. Josiah Ward ran a grist mill and a saw mill.

- In 1809, Josiah Ward also erected the first cider mill.

- In 1811, Sylvester Tinker put up a tannery west of town. John Goss, Rufus Belding, Reuben Upson, Jonathon Foster, and Abel Sabin assembled to elect township officers: Samuel Hale, Reuben Upson, and Rufus Belding were elected trustees. Several persons were appointed to township positions: Nehemiah Bacon and Raphael Hurlburt were appointed as Overseers of the Poor, and Joshua Hollister and Abel Sabin as Fence Viewers. Thomas Hale was appointed as Appraiser. Timothy Culver was selected as Lister of Taxable-property, and Arad Upson as Constable. Martin Kent, Ezekiel Tupper, Ebenezer Cutler, E. Merriman, and A. Upson were appointed as Supervisors while Mosses Adams, Thomas Hale, John Goss, E. Cutler, John Sabin, Bradford Waldo, E. Merriman, T. Culver, J. Hollister, Ephraim Sabin, A. Upson, Schoby Outcalt, and David Ticknor were Jurors. Jonathan Foster was made Justice of the Peace.

- In 1812, David James, Samuel Redfeld, William Thornton, and Elisha Ward went to the War of 1812. The Congregational Church was officially organized and had 15 members. Deacon Festus Spellman and wife, Roxy Spellman, Mr. William Jones, and Deacon James Coe were active church members.

- In 1814, a Methodist group was organized by Reverend Ira Eddy.

- In 1818, an epidemic of terrible fever caused the deaths of many Randolph Township residents.

- In 1819, a Baptist church with 12 members was organized.

- In 1820, the first post office was established with Oliver Dickinson as Post Master.

- In 1828, a Disciples Church was organized, but their church wasn't built until 1860.

- In 1829, a Catholic Church was founded by the Germans and organized by Reverend Victor Housner. The first active priest was Reverend Matthias Wertz in 1838. (Note: Chapter II, paragraph 5, indicates a different year and priest for St. Joseph's. As stated in the introduction, some references provide conflicting information.)

- In 1832, the Congregationalists built their first church.

- In 1833, the Methodists built their first church.

- In the mid 1850s, Randolph was a station for the Underground Railroad.

- In 1857, the German Reformed Church was founded in the township.

- In 1861, 180 soldiers served in the Civil War.

The Rootstown Area, Early 19th Century

- In <u>1800</u>, Ephraim Root, Harvey Davenport, and Nathaniel Cook from Connecticut arrived to begin surveying Town 2 Range 8 into 48 lots.
- In <u>1801</u>, David Root (brother to Ephraim Root) and Yale graduate Nathan Muzzy came to Rootstown.
- In <u>1802</u>, Henry O'Neill and family and Samuel McCoy arrived from Ireland. McCoy was uneducated, but was an accomplished fiddler. Henry became Justice of the Peace and served five years. He also erected the first distillery. John McCoy (son of Samuel McCoy) was given 50 acres by Root because he was the first born child of the township. Michael Hirtle and Frederick Caris came from Pennsylvania.
- In <u>1803</u>, John Caris and Arthur Anderson also came. Caris and his wife settled at Muddy (now Hodgson) Lake.
- In <u>1804</u>, John Caris's father, Frederick Caris, Thaddeus Andrews, Nathan Chapman and his son Ephraim, Jacob-Charles and Abraham Reed, and Hannah Russell came from Connecticut. Mr. Root erected the first frame barn with the help of David Wright of Ravenna who hewed the timber and Nathan Muzzy who framed it.
- In <u>1805</u>, Beeman Chapman (brother to Ephraim Chapman) and his wife arrived. Stephen Colton and family came from Connecticut.

Note: A treaty council held at Fort Industry nullified the Indian claims to this area of land. There was then less fear of Indians, and settlers came in increased numbers.

- In <u>1806</u>, Gersham Bostwick and his parents, Mr. and Mrs. Edmund Bostwick, came. When Edmund was over 80 years old, he made a trip to Philadelphia from Rootstown and back again. Alpheus and Samuel Andreous along with Martin Bissell arrived with their families. A niece of Andrews, Miss Mary Whitney, and a team driver, Gersham Norris, came. Mother Ward also came this year but without her husband. As stated earlier, she could do the work of any man, and one day walked from Rootstown to Poland, some 40 miles.
- In <u>1807</u>, Hiram Roundy, his wife and adopted son, G.H. Prindle, came. Heman Bostwick and Titus Belding also came. Robert McKnight, his wife, mother, only son Robert Jr., James Alcorn and William Alcorn also arrived.
- In <u>1807-08</u>, the first school cabin was built at the town center. The teacher was Samuel Andrews. Miss Polly Harman taught after Samuel.
- In <u>1808</u>, Ebenezer Bostwick and family came and started a pottery. Ephraim Root built a sawmill north of town. Phillip Willard and Valentine Coosard also came. Ariel Case and John Wright sowed a cleared area to wheat.
- In <u>1809</u>, Titus Belding married Lucy, daughter of Gersham Bostwick. Nathan Chapman died and was the first person to be buried in the burial grounds near the center. Israel Coe and William and Chauncey Newbury came.
- In <u>1810</u>, Merriam Richardson and David Parker along with their families arrived. Daniel and Reuben Hall and their sister Eliza, who married Gersham Norris, came. James Wright

came in 1810. He was appointed as the first Post Master in <u>1821</u> and served for 20 years. Otis Reed was later appointed as Post Master. Rev. Giles H. Cowles organized the Congregational Church. The township was organized in this year.

- In <u>1811</u>, Samuel B. Spellman and Asa Seymour came from Massachusetts. Asher Gurley came from Connecticut. Robert J. Collins Sr. and his sons Robert J., David, and Daniel arrived with their families.
- In <u>1812</u>, the trustees were Gersham Bostwick, Frederick Caris Jr., and Thaddeus Andrews. The Clerk was Alpheus Andrews. Samuel Andrews was the Justice of the Peace.
- In <u>1814</u>, Rev. Henry Shewell came and in <u>1815</u> organized the <u>Methodist Episcopal Church</u>. Rev. Ira Eddy was its first Pastor.
- In <u>1819</u>, William Huffman and Thomas Hayden came.
- In <u>1850</u>, Rootstown had approximately 7,104 acres in cultivation, 7,560 in woodland, and 2,091 in wasteland—a total of 17,175 acres.
- In <u>1884</u>, a two story school building was erected at a cost of $3,400.00. It was located near the Methodist Church just south of the town center. A general store at New Milford (a settlement two miles to the east) was organized by L.F. Pike. A grist mill had been established years before and operated by F.P. Root. C.H. Bradshaw operated a sawmill south of Rootstown. Jacob Kriss operated a wagon and carriage shop years before at New Milford. Sandy Lake, Muddy Lake (now known as Hodgson), Muzzy Lake and Ward's Pond were favorite gathering places.
- In <u>1885</u>, the Rootstown Protective Association, an insurance company, was organized: G.W. Bow was President; H.M. Deming was Vice President; H.O. Reed was Secretary; and C.H. Bradshaw was Treasurer. David Bogue, Homer Chapman, and Elam Underwood were Directors. The amount of insurance in force was $480,963. This company went out of business in 1934.

See Chapter XI (Document Section, Map #2 & Map #3) for 1874 maps of Randolph and Rootstown Townships.

This author makes no attempt to develop fully the history of Portage County or the townships including the townships of Rootstown and Randolph. Therefore, this chapter is but an abbreviation of the growth of Portage County and especially of the townships of Randolph and Rootstown. It was included in this book to set the stage for the establishment of the two Roman Catholic churches now serving the Catholics of these two communities.

It should be understood that few Catholics came to the Rootstown area when it was first settled. They were drawn to the fertile farmland in the southwest of the county. The rest of this book will be dedicated to the history and development of St. Joseph's and St. Peter's Catholic Churches.

Chapter II
Establishment of St. Joseph's Catholic Church, Randolph

This chapter contains a chronological list of the priests who served at St. Joseph's, Randolph, certain immigration interests, particular parishioner concerns of their church and school, and selected stories as they were relayed to this author by parishioners.

In the early pioneer days of the Randolph, Ohio, area between 1831 and 1834, some thirty Catholic families came from Alsace-Loraine in France and the Hessian States of Germany. These Catholics were under the Diocese of Cincinnati, Ohio, which was established in 1821.

Some of these early Catholics were Adam Kline, John Adam Kline, John Berlin, John Luli, J. Weiss, Anthony Weber, George Horning, Anthony Miller, Nicholas Knapp, Christopher Fisher, John Gauer, John Heisler, Peter Knapp, Adam Schweigert, and Adam Winkler. These are all well-known family names, families that were instrumental in the development of the Randolph area and St. Joseph's. Other family names will surface throughout this book.

In the early part of the nineteenth century, there was a custom among the Hessian people of the southwestern German states to divide their agricultural lands among their heirs. Soon land became scarce and crowded. This scarcity of land caused some of the Hessians to migrate to the United States. Social, financial, and revolutionary movements in Germany were also causes of migration.

Father John Martin Henni

In 1830, Father John Martin Henni, who was ordained February 2, 1829, and was from Switzerland, visited Randolph. Father Henni spoke German, French, and English, and said Mass in various homes in the area. The first Mass said that is recorded was in the home of Anthony Miller. Father Henni was pastor for a short time at St. John's, Canton, and was appointed pastor at St. Joseph's in 1831. He did not stay very long, however, since he was sent to Cincinnati soon after his arrival. In 1881, Father Henni became Bishop of Milwaukee. Father Henni also served other area churches such as St. Mary's in Morges, Carroll County. Father Henni built a 40' x 60' log chapel at St. Mary's which was the beginning of the parish. Later on, Father Henni became Vicar General of Cincinnati Arch-diocese and the first Bishop of Milwaukee. Many of the early priests were like circuit riders and covered large areas where Catholics had settled.

JOSEPH SCHROEDER
First School Teacher, 1832

Another early Catholic settler was Franz Adam Knapp who came from Wald Erlenbach Hessen, Germany, in 1836. He donated land in the Randolph area (research does not reveal exact location) where a log schoolhouse was built that lasted until 1835. As stated in Chapter I, this school is believed to be the first parochial school west of the Alleghenies. Its first teacher, Joseph Schroeder, was the great-grandfather of present St. Peter's parishioner Henry J. Kline, a prominent Rootstown cattle and grain farmer.

In 1855, another Catholic school was built south of Randolph at an area called Beachland. Reference to this school is listed in the archives of St. Mary's, Morges, and in the interview of Irene Lang May, a parishioner of St. Joseph's, Randolph. It was too far, however, for children to travel from the St. Joseph area, so the school was abandoned in 1897. There are few official records as to the operation of this school; therefore, very little is known about it.

The establishment of the first Catholic school in the Randolph area (1831) clearly shows the area was well ahead of the settlements of Kent and Ravenna, farther to the north in Portage County. These settlements did not have Catholic schools until 1881 and 1886 respectively. Several historical references listed in this book state that the first church building was of log construction and was built in 1835. It should be noted, however, that the *Pioneer History Book (1802-1865)* suggests that two Catholic churches were built about this time, one for the French and one for the German people.

The Catholic Telegraph of Cincinnati (the oldest Catholic newspaper in the United States), first published on October 22, 1830, had an article dated September 11, 1835, which reported that Bishop John Baptist Purcell visited Randolph. Purcell followed Bishop Edward Fenwick 1821-1832 as the second Bishop of Cincinnati. See Chapter XI (Photo Section, Photos #1-#13) for a complete list of Bishops and their photos. The article stated that the Bishop visited many Catholics and reported on forty-five families. This first church or churches of 1835 and the school house of 1831 served these forty-five families from Randolph, Suffield, and Rootstown areas. The church was a mission church of St. John's, Canton, Ohio, approximately twenty miles to the south, and later of St. Louis, Louisville, Ohio, approximately twenty miles to the southeast.

The Randolph church was referred to in the *Catholic Telegraph* as the Church of St. Martin, located about one mile from Randolph center. The exact location cannot be established since the reports at the time mentioned the church at Suffield and Randolph. It should also be mentioned that, at various times, the present church at St. Joseph's was referred to as St. Martin's, St. Joseph's, and St. Sebastian's.

The reference to St. Martin is of special interest and appears to be accurate information since it came from the *Catholic Telegraph* after Bishop Purcell had returned to Cincinnati. There was a St. Martin's Church at Valley City some thirty miles to the west in Medina County, but it was known as Queen of All Saints during Purcell's visit to Randolph. St. Martin was a logical name for the Randolph church since Father John Martin Henni had been in charge there in 1831, celebrating Mass in various homes.

In 1841, the *Catholic Telegraph* reported a second visit by Bishop Purcell. A second church building had been constructed in 1838, but soon after completion, burned to the ground. There was much infighting between the parishioners as to where the replacement church should be located and whether English or German should be used for church singing. Bishop Purcell stated in the *Catholic Telegraph,* "Some base incendiary caused the fire." The *Catholic Telegraph* reported that the Bishop knelt and cried.

The Diocese of Cleveland book, titled *A History of Catholicity in Northern Ohio and in the Diocese of Cleveland* (1903), clearly states that Catholics from Rootstown burned the church because they did not like the 1838 location. This statement was based on information from Bishop Purcell.

It is not certain which family, but either the Knapp or Miller family, immediately built another church of log construction. This church, however, was never completed or used because of the constant infighting of the parishioners.

In the 1841 visit by Bishop Purcell, the Bishop and Father John Martin Henni (who was at that time assigned to Cincinnati) went to the uncompleted church. The *Catholic Telegraph* referred to this as a visit to St. Martin's, Randolph. On November 19, 1841, Father Henni preached a long and affecting sermon about honesty and Catholicism.

On their way home to Cincinnati, by way of Canton, the priests intercepted Father John Nepomucene Neuman who was a priest from the Congregation of the Most Holy Redeemer. He was 5'4", of Bohemian descent, and spoke German, Greek, Latin, Bohemian, Slavic, English, Italian, French, and Spanish. He had arrived in New York in 1836 aboard the steamer *Europa*. It was a cold and rainy night, and Purcell and Henni rode in an open carriage. Bishop Purcell attempted to talk Father Neuman into becoming a secular priest and taking over St. Martin's at Randolph. Father Neuman had reunited several disillusioned Catholics at St. Alphonsus at Peru near Norwalk, Ohio, back to the Catholic Church, and Purcell knew this was the priest for Randolph. Father Neuman refused the offer but did go to Randolph for a ten-day mission where he preached twice a day, heard 300 confessions, prayed the Rosary, and gave Communion to 100 people.

The third church, completed in 1845, was referred to in national directories from 1846-1848 as St. Sebastian's of Suffield. There was no church at Suffield, so it is logical to conclude that the records meant Randolph.

In 1852, Father Neuman was appointed the fourth Bishop of Philadelphia. He was canonized June 19, 1977, by Pope Paul VI, and became the first American male citizen to be so canonized. See Chapter XI (Photo Section, Photo #69) for St. John Neumann & Chapter XI (Report Section, Report #15) for The Life of St. John Neumann.

The following is a list of priests and some of their accomplishments at St. Joseph's, Randolph. There are some missing church records and some assignments were over-lapping. Additionally, photos of certain early priests could not be located.

- 1829—A different source states that a Catholic church was established served by Fathers Victor Housner and Matthias Wertz.
- 1831—Father John Martin Henni said Masses in various homes. Father Henni also accompanied Bishop Purcell on visits to Randolph.
- 1836-37—Father F. Hoffman, D.D., originally from the Alsace-Loraine region in France, served as pastor. Father Hoffman was a missionary priest from Canton, Ohio. Records indicate that he was assisted at times by Father M. Werz of Canton and Father J. Alemany.
- 1838—Father Matthias provided Catholic services, and between 1838 and 1840, twenty-five children were baptized.
- 1841-1842—Father Peter McLaughlin served. Note: He is not listed with the other priests in the parish history who served at St. Joseph's, but is named in Father W.A. Jurgen's *Diocese of Cleveland History* as serving from 1841-1842. Jurgen's history was not published until 1980.
- 1842-1843—Father Basil Schorb, from Doylestown, Wayne County, served the needs of

the Randolph Catholics.

- 1844—Father Francis DeSales Brunner served. A new church was constructed at St. Joseph's at this time (1844-45). Brunnerdale Seminary, Canton, Ohio, was named after Father Brunner.
- 1845—Father John Wittmer was pastor. The first parish house was built during this time. Frs. J. Ringely and P. Capeder also assisted Father Wittmer.
- 1847-1848—Father John Luhr from Canton, OH, was pastor. (Rev. Amadeus Rappe was Bishop from 1847-1870 of the Cleveland Diocese.) The Cleveland Diocese was established in 1847, and St. Joseph's Catholic Church was now part of that Diocese.
- 1848-1851—Father P. Weber served as resident pastor.
- 1851-1857—Father George Stein, from Baden, Germany, was pastor.

- 1857-1861—Father John Hackspeil, from Tyrol, Austria, served. St. Joseph's was steadily growing and there was talk of building a larger church, but the Civil War started in 1861 and the parish decided not to build. Note: 1858--Randolph Fair starts.

FATHER JOHN HACKSPIEL
1857-1861

FATHER VICTOR HAUSSNER
1861-1868

- 1861-1868—Father Victor Haussener served. A new church, 50'x 100', was constructed in 1865, at a cost of $1,700. It is the same style of St. Peter's church built in 1868 at Rootstown.

- 1868-1869—Father Herbstritt was pastor. St. Peter's Catholic Church in Rootstown was built during his tenure and under his direction.

FATHER HERBSTRITT
1868-1869

FATHER J. KOEHN
1869-1875

- 1869-1875—Father J. Koehn served as pastor. (Rev. Richard Gilmour was Bishop of Cleveland Diocese, 1872-1891.)

- 1875-1885—Father N. Kirch served as pastor.

FATHER NICHOLAS KIRCH
1875-1885

- 1885-1891—Father Sylvan Rebholz served. He arranged for Sisters of Notre Dame to establish a convent and teach in the school at St. Joseph's. The present parish house was built in 1887.

Father Sylvan Rebholz

- 1891—Father J.P. Golden served until November of this year.

- 1891-1892—Father J. Romer was pastor. (Rev. Ignatious Horstman was Bishop of the Cleveland Diocese, 1892-1908.)

FATHER JOHN THEIN,
1892-1903.

- 1892-1903—Father J. Thein was pastor.

- 1903-1910—Father George Vogt was pastor. It was during this time, in 1904 to be exact, the church burned. The only thing saved was the Blessed Sacrament by Father Vogt. The seventh church was built in that same year at a cost of $60,000 dollars and stands as a beautiful tribute to German influence of stone and brick construction. It was dedicated June 25, 1905, by Bishop Schremes. This church looks much like St. Peter's Church in Heppenheim, Germany, ancestral home to many St. Joseph families. See Chapter XI (Photo Section, Photos #14 & #15) for photos of both churches. (Rev. John Farrely was Bishop of the Cleveland Diocese, 1909-1921.)

Father George Vogt

- 1910-1926—Father George Reber was pastor. (Rev. Joseph Schremes was Bishop, 1921-1943.)

Father George Reber

- 1927-1928—Father Edward Spitzig was pastor. In an exchange of letters with Bishop Schremes, he gained permission to build a shrine like the famous shrine at Lourdes, France, on the grounds of Joseph's. Father told the bishop that he dreamed about it day and night. The bishop said he would give his permission, but it had to be an exact replica of Lourdes. The Shrine to Our Lady was built in a gravel pit a few hundred feet to the north of the church on August 14, 1927. This grotto is a replica of Lourdes Massabielle, France, where the Blessed Virgin Mary appeared 18 times to Bernadette Soubirous. St. Bernadette was beatified in 1925. A Mass, the Rosary, and a candlelight procession are held each year at the shrine at St. Joseph's. It is called the tritium. People attend from other parishes including St. Peter of the Fields.

Our Lady of Lourdes Grotto in France

Our Lady of Lourdes Grotto at St. Joseph

Certain members of St. Peter's, Rootstown, helped in the construction of the grotto. One such parishioner was the author's father, John Lawrence Winkler. He told the story that as a young man, age 24, he pushed wheelbarrow-loads of cement up the hill to the top of the Grotto. Joseph Paulus—St. Joseph parishioner and grandfather to Henry J. Kline—used horses and a slip-scraper to move the dirt around. Carl Shaffer and George Mercer were St. Joseph parishioners who also worked on the Grotto. Construction machinery of the 21st Century was obviously not known at that time. Many other Catholic men from both parishes assisted in the building of this beautiful shrine to Our Blessed Lady. See Chapter XI (Photo Section, Photo #17) for a photo of the 1926 construction of this shrine.

Father Spitzig died unexpectedly after one and one-half years at St. Joseph's. When he came to St. Joseph's he brought a large collection of relics from miscellaneous saints and they were displayed during the Masses. It was reported that the number of relics was eighty-five.

Side altar and Fr. Spitzig's relics at St. Joseph's, 1927-1928

16

- 1928--Father Franz Feinler then served a short time as interim pastor until Father Frederick Bertram came in 1928.

- 1928-1956--Father Bertran fostered and advertised the new Grotto and soon bus-loads of people came from wide areas to visit and pray. Cures and favors from Our Lady

Father Frederick Bertram

were reported but were never proven. Special Masses are said to this day at the site. (The Youngstown Diocese was established in 1943; Rev. James A. McFadden served as Bishop, 1943-1952.) Father Bertran died on June 17, 1956, after serving for 28 years at St. Joseph's, longer than any other priest. Father was a large man and assisted anyone who was in need. He had a habit of picking up young children who would visit him by their cheeks. The author knows this to be true because he experienced it himself when he was a young lad and on a visit with his father to the rectory. (Rev. Emmet M. Walsh was Bishop, 1952-1968.)

- 1956-1961—Father Ed Dierker served as pastor. During this time, Mr. Frank Lang retired as the church organist. Frank had served in that capacity for 54 years.

Father John Pertz

- 1961-1967—Father John Pertz served as pastor. During this time, the St. Joseph Catholic War Veterans Post, started by Father Bertran, placed a statue of St. Francis of Assisi, Patron of Servicemen, behind the school building. (Rev. James W. Malone was Bishop of the Youngstown Diocese, 1968-1995.)

- 1967-1972—Monsignor Joseph Galganski served as pastor. Vatican II was taking place at this time and because of changes made in the Universal Roman Catholic Church, the beautiful majestic altars at the front of the church were removed. Their removal upset many parishioners, and the older ones still voice their displeasure today. Monsignor Galganski was an artist and painted many pictures of St. Joseph's Church and grounds. See Chapter XI (Photo Section, Photo #16) for photo of the majestic main altar.

- 1972-1977—Father Timothy Kenney, an Irish priest, served the parish. During this time the first Parish Council was established. Father Kenny truly had the leprechaun smile and quick wit. Monsignor Glenn Holbrook came during this time and assisted Father Kenney with parish duties. Monsignor taught art classes to the children and adults.

Father Timothy E. Kenney

Father Joseph Martin

- 1977-1982—Father Joseph Martin served the parish. Father added a kindergarten to the school program. Once at a funeral Mass, Father Martin said to the grieving family, "Peace will come, but you must wait for it." This author was present when Father made that statement. Father Martin loved to work in the church gardens and smoke his cigar.

- 1982-1985—Father John P. Ashton was the pastor. Deacons and priests from the Youngstown Diocese gathered in the Knights of Columbus hall for a celebration where Father fell on a wet hall floor and broke his leg. He soon healed and served the parish well.

- 1985-1986—Father Robert Novotny served the parish. In 1986, the RCIA (Rite of Christian Initiation) program was begun.

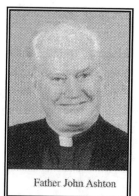

Father John Ashton

Father Gerald Curran

- 1986—Father Gerald Curran served as administrator for a short time. He loved the children and would bring them up around the altar during Mass so they could observe what he was doing.

- 1987-1995—Father Thomas Dyer served the parish. Father was responsible for starting several social activities like golf outings, aerobics classes, a food shelf, and the recycling center.

Father Thomas Dyer

- 1995—Father Edward Wieczorek became pastor. Shortly after Father's appointment, he left for six months to study in Rome. Father John Murray served until his return from Rome. Father Wieczorek is a very humble, prayerful, and traditional priest. The parish thrives today with approximately 900 families. The placement of spotlights illuminate this beautiful brick and stone structure at night, and one can truly feel a majestic presence of this church at St. Joseph's, Randolph, Ohio. (Rev. Thomas J. Tobin served as Bishop of the Youngstown Diocese from 1996-2005.)

St. Joseph's is the oldest Catholic parish in Portage County, and at the time of its conception, it was the sixth oldest Catholic parish in Ohio.

Father Wieczorek continues to be the parish pastor at this writing (2010). In 1997-1998, a half-million dollar exterior-interior renovation was done to the church. It goes without saying that this church, grotto, cemetery, and school setting are one of beauty. (Reverend George Murray was appointed Bishop of the Youngstown Diocese on January 30, 2007 by Pope Benedict XVI.)

Priests, Brothers, Deacons and Sisters from St. Joseph's;

Priests, Brothers, Deacons from St. Peter's:
1892- Father Joseph M. Paulus
1903- Father George Lang
1904- Father Joseph Horning
1918- Father Edmund Rhodes
1954- Father Fred Lang
1954- Father Paul Wohlwend
1955- Father Carl Wise
1956- Father James Schrader
1975- Father James Lang
1976- Father Ernest Krantz
1925- Brother James H. Kline
1982- Permanent Deacon James White
1991- Permanent Deacon Thomas Shay

Sisters from our Parish:
Notre Dame Sisters

Emma Horning- Sister Mary Clementia
Elizabeth Horning- Sister Mary Fortunata
Julia Paulus- Sister Mary Roberta
Appolonia Lang- Sister Mary Alice
Martha Lang- Sister Mary Isabel
Gertrude Horning- Sister Mary Dolora
Helen Rhodes- Sister Mary George
Catherine Koerber- Sister Mary Winfred
Elenora Horning- Sister Mary Martha
Cecilia Wise- Sister Mary Dorotheus
Agnes Wohlwend- Sister Mary Verone
Mary Moldor- Sister Mary Clareen
Victoria May- Sister Mary Cordilia
Mary May- Sister Mary Damian
Bertha Paulus- Sister Mary Deotila
Hilda Trares- Sister Mary Corleen
Stella Horning- Sister Mary Amanda

Helen Moledor- Sister Mary Roseann
Dorothy Eichler- Sister Mary Clementine
Grace Koby- Sister Mary Wilbert
Loretta Strahler- Sister Mary Merita
Catherina Kehner- Sister Mary Caron
Dorothy Strahler- Sister Mary Doreen
Mildred Monter- Sister Mary Joanita
Barbara Klodt- Sister Mary Barbara
Theresa Dugan- Sister Mary Theresa
Ruth Koby- Sister Mary Ruth

Benedictine Sisters
Bertha Horning- Sister Mary Adele

Poor Clares
Barbara Klein- Sister Mary Ildephonsa

Medical Mission Sisters
Edna Strahler- Sister Mary Sylvia

Sisters of Humility of Mary
Josephine Rettig- Sister Mary Cresentia
Joanne Bormet- Sister Mary Joanne

Franciscan Sisters
Anna Dussel- Sister Mary Constantia
Mary Eichler- Sister Mary Thadea
Louise Harter- Sister Mary Regina

Sisters of St. Dominic
Agnes Paulus- Sister Mary Rosalia
Alice Horning- Sister Mary Yvonne

Sisters of Charity of St. Augustin
Gertrude Rothermel- Sister Mary Eulalia
Mary Pero- Sister Margare Mary

Several of the nuns were transported to St. Peter's in the 1940s to teach in the CCD program. Deacon Thomas Shay is presently a Deacon at St. Peter of the Fields (2010).

Chapter III
Establishment of St. Peter's
Catholic Church, Rootstown

This chapter will be dedicated to the thirty-three priests and two deacons who served St. Peter's plus significant parishioners who left their mark on the parish during its 141 years of existence. Two nuns also came from the parish and served in various religious capacities during their careers. A third sister served as parish administrator for a time. Proper names of these priests, deacons, nuns, and special parishioners and the years they served will be listed throughout this chapter. It is the hope of this author that the stories of those persons selected will provide special meaning and purpose to the reader.

St. Peter's Catholic Church in Rootstown was built in 1868-1869 by farmers and craftsmen from the surrounding area. Since the Civil War veterans from Rootstown had just returned home from the war, it is most likely that they also assisted. See the last page of this book for a picture of the parish house and Church dated 1900.

Fr. John J. Boyle
1898 - 1900

The church was a mission church of St. Joseph's, Randolph, and their pastor, Rev. A. Herbstritt, supervised the construction. Other priests also served St. Peter's coming from St. John's Cathedral, Cleveland, Ohio, and the Blessed Sacrament Fathers coming from Canton, Ohio. St. Peter's remained a mission church for thirty years until the assignment of its first resident pastor, Father John Boyle, in 1898.

More specifically, priests who served St. Peter's from 1868 to 1898 were Father Herbstritt, 1868; Father J. Koehn, 1869; Father Nicholas Kirch, 1875; Father Sylvan Rebholz, 1885; Fr, Joseph Romer; 1891; and Father John Thein, 1892.

In the later years of the 1950s and thereafter, priests assisted as administrators or liturgical or canonical pastors from Brunnerdale Seminary and Central Catholic, Canton, Ohio. Some also came from the Society of St. Paul, Canfield, Ohio. They will be identified later in this chapter with the actual years they served.

On December 31, 1866, one acre of land was deeded to church trustees Adam Kline, Francis Gauer, Martin Miller, Michael Bills, and George Gouthier by Adam and Catherine Winkler for $100. Adam Winkler served in the Mexican War of 1846. Now we begin to see the same family names as those of early Catholics in Randolph.

In 1868, a 30'x 55' Gothic style framed building was constructed at a cost of $1,200. This building is the church one can see today positioned in the same place as it was built 141 years ago. The church had two rooms—one for Mass and sacraments, and the other for catechism. A larger front entrance and an addition on the back to the north were accomplished in 1947-1948.

As already stated, the first resident pastor was Father John Boyle, born in Philadelphia, Pennsylvania, October 13, 1848, and ordained February 27, 1892. He was a professor at the Philadelphia Seminary, served as assistant at Pottsville, New York, and at St. Theresa and St. Joachim in Shandon, Pennsylvania. He then came to Cleveland in 1887 and served as an assistant at St. John's Cathedral until he was assigned to St. Peter's on January 1, 1898. He served until

June 1900 and was then transferred to East Palestine where he remained until his death in December of 1900.

When Father Boyle came to St. Peter's, the church had 45 families and was part of the Cleveland Diocese. Father had the Infant of Prague statue sent to St. Peter's where it is still displayed today in the original church. More information on this statue and its history is included further on in this chapter. For Father's order of events for First Communion on October 1, 1899, see Chapter XI (Document Section, Document #4).

What was it like at St. Peter's during the pastorate of Father John Boyle, the first priest?

Several excerpts were taken from Father Boyle's announcement book of 1900. He reports that nominees for councilmen were Henry Kline, George Biltz, Nich Knapp, and Jim Heisler. Henry Kline was selected by a two-vote majority. The tellers of the election were Adam Reis and Charles Miller. The spelling of Reis is interesting; today the Reis descendents spell their name *Rice.*

Father reports that the pews in the center of the church would seat four persons, and three persons on the side aisles. This spacing is much different than the pew arrangement in the historic church today. Single seats were rented for six dollars per year. Father cautioned that families who had children who would make their First Communion were expected to pay for the necessary number of seats. Father said that Councilmen Henry Kline and John Lansinger "will auction off" the seats to the highest bidder. Father Boyle speaks of the more than 115 seats remaining unrented, but admits they wouldn't all be rented because the parish did not have that many people. He says, however, that there had been "a wonderful increase in membership during the past twelve months," and that he would soon read the names of those who had paid their pew rent.

Father reports that the church was through with the building operations including the church and rectory; therefore, the only expense the parishioners would have "is the current expense and the pastor's salary."

The parishioners were told to bring in one or two pounds of wax candles for blessing. Some candles would remain at the church, and some would go back home for sick calls, etc. The candles for the church had to be wax and plentiful since many were used for Forty Hours' Devotion and other liturgical feast days. Father announced that the feast of St. Blasius was on February 3, and there would be a low Mass and throats would be blessed. He told the story of the young boy with a bone in his throat and that the doctors had given up on him. As the boy was choking to death, St. Blasius prayed over him and the boy lived.

Father mentions that Henry Dussel, Henry Kline, Adam Reis, Mrs. Luli, and Mrs. Paulus did some work in the church. He also announces on several occasions that the children's choir would sing at certain Masses. Father speaks of "evil-minded persons who despised and hated the parishioners" and who had predicted a year ago that the parish would not last six months. He states that these people did all they could to destroy the church, but they failed. Father says that the parishioners built a new church, bought land, and built a house for the priest. He also said these "evil-minded" persons have continued their malicious opposition to the parish. Father says, "They want us to fail, but that will never happen as long as I am here, and what I say is the truth. They will hide their faces in shame."

Obviously there was a serious problem at St. Peter's in 1900, and Father Boyle was determined to keep the parish together.

Father explains what Septuajesima Sunday means. The word means "seventy," and in the early years of the Church, the faithful fasted for seventy days before Easter. Then the church reduced the seventy days to sixty, then to fifty days, and finally to forty days as it is today (2010). This reduction in the number of fasting days was done, according to Father Boyle, by Pope Gregory and Pope Gelasius.

Father reports that he could not sprinkle Holy Water over the church and congregation because he did not have the correct High Mass vestments called "the Copes." But he says he now has the vestments of different colors so the sprinkling of Holy Water would be done the next Sunday, which would be the second Sunday of Lent, 1900.

On February 21, 1900, the Rt. Rev. Bishop G.F. Houk, Chancellor of the Cleveland Diocese at that time, sent out the regulations for Lent. This author was struck by how different they were from today's regulations. Please see Chapter XI (Document Section, Document #5) for these regulations.

Father reports that a German priest was coming for those who wanted to go to confession in German before Easter. He also says parishioners may confess in English if they would only try it once! He probably added this statement because most of the parishioners chose to speak German, not English, at that time. He speaks of wine and Florida palms coming to the Rootstown railroad station in time for Palm Sunday.

Father reports that anyone who gave fifty cents or more for the special collection would have their names published. Compare these amounts to today's contributions. The report for the first Sunday after Easter reads as follows:

Adam Lansinger $1.00	Adam Bower $.50
John C. Kline $1.00	Mrs. Adam Winkler $.50
Michael Biltz $1.00	Martin Kline $.50
Mrs. George Kline $1.00	George Kline $.50
Charles Luli $1.00	Mrs. George Kline $.50
William Pitz $1.00	John Redinger $.50
Frank Marquart $1.00	Wallace Winkler $.50
Charles Winkler $1.00	George Marquart $.50
Charles Kline $.75	Miss Anna Fleishman $.50
Henry Kline $.50	Adam Fleishman $.50
Joseph Heisler $.50	Lawrence Knapp $.50
John Biltz $.50	Henry C. Kline $.50
Miss Mary Marquart $.50	Mrs. Elizabeth Miller $.50
Miss Eva Palm $.50	Mrs. John B. Kline $.50
Mrs. R. Doyle $.50	Mrs. John C. Kline $.50
Nicholas Knapp $.50	Mrs. Martin Miller $.50
Miss Kate Miller $.50	George Biltz $.50
Adam Reis $.50	Smaller Contributions Totaled $4.81

GRAND TOTAL: $26.56 (which was $1.84 more than the previous year)!

These names identify the core families at St. Peter's in its formative years, and in many cases, the descendants of these families are represented today at St. Peter's.

Father Boyle describes a situation concerning the deterioration of the parish grounds. He states that the grounds around the parish house and church were seeded in the fall, but because the horses and wagons drove over the area between the church and parish house so many times, "The grass has died out and the area looks very bad." He says he spent $1.60 of his own money for grass seed in the past, but can't do it again. He asks that four or five parishioners tear up the ground, put in some new soil, and seed it. If they don't, he says, he will have it done and charge it to the congregation. He reports later that John B. Kline, Joseph Heisler, and Adam Reis fixed the lawn.

During the third Sunday of Easter, 1900, Father speaks about the unveiling and blessing of the new image of the miraculous Infant of Prague at St. Peter's. He says that he does not believe there is another statue of this kind in any church in the entire diocese. He says devotion to the Infant of Prague has existed in Austria, Germany, and elsewhere in Europe for more than two centuries. He explains that the statue came from Munich, Germany, and was taken to the city of Prague, Bohemia, and touched to the original miraculous image in the parish church of Our Lady of Victories. He tells the parishioners to bring their friends and relatives of other churches to see the statue.

The following is a quote taken from Father Boyle's own 1900 announcement book:

Immediately after the May devotion and before Benediction this afternoon, we will have the peculiar and very pretty service of the unveiling and blessing of a new image of the miraculous Infant of Prague. Das ginaden vickie prayer oder das wander thaetige.

I don't think that there is another statue of this kind in any church in the whole Diocese and Rootstown's Church will have the honor of introducing this beautiful devotion which has existed in Austria and Germany and elsewhere in Europe during more than two centuries.

Whilst I have been particularly moved to secure this image for the sake of children of the parish among whom I wish to spread vocation to the infant Jesus, I want to say to their parents and all the grown people of the congregation that the devotion to the miraculous Infant of Prague is practiced by all classes of people in the old country.

Our statue has come from the old country, Munich, and before it was exported here it was taken to the city of Prague in Bohemia and there it was brought in contact, in touch, with the original miraculous Image in the parish church of Our Lady of Victories. I have distributed during the past year among the SS children a large number of leaflets containing a picture of the Infant of Prague, a short history of it, and its veneration, and also some prayers to be said before it. I have several hundred more of these leaflets and I would be pleased to distribute them among the older folks. I suppose I have at least a couple hundred of these leaflets printed in the German language for those who would prefer them in German rather than in English. You all have friends too in other parishes and I will be also pleased to give you all some copies in both English and German for your friends. I am sure that many not belonging to our Congregation will be anxious to come and see our Image when they hear of its being set up in our Rootstown Church.

I trust that all of you will endeavor to be present this afternoon when we have ceremony of unveiling the statue and dedicating ourselves and our parish to the Infant Jesus of Prague.

--Occurred 3rd Sunday after Easter-

I shall probably have something to say then about the history of the original Image, together with an explanation of the devotion and a reference to the many and recent miracles that have been wrought through prayer before it.

Additional information on this statue can be found in Chapter VII.

During Father Boyle's time at St. Peter's, he made many requests for pew rent. That is where his salary and operating revenue came from, very different than today's method of Church finances and support.

On the fourth Sunday after Easter, his report indicates that George Biltz, Henry Kline, Adam Lansinger, Nicholas Knapp, Adam Fleishman, John C. Kline, Adam Winkler, Lawrence Knapp, Joseph Heisler, Adam Bower, Frank Marquart, Elizabeth Miller, John B. Kline, Wallace Winkler, Albert Mitch, John Dussel, George Kline, Mrs. Peter Dussel, Adam Basil, Adam Reis, M. Miller, Martin Kline, Michael Biltz, Vincent Basil, Adam Knapp, Miss Mary Marquart, George Marquart, Mrs. Bentz, Mrs. Katie Reis, Mrs. Katherine Zeller, Mrs. R. Doyle, Mrs. Barbara Kline, Michael Isenberg, W.G. Biltz, and John Biltz paid their pew rent.

These names are listed so that the reader can see that there are a few new names that come up that are not listed on the preceding pages concerning the Easter collection. Remember, Father said the church was growing with new members.

Father speaks of Rogation Days (which means the "supplications as chanted during procession on the three days before Ascension Day). He said this was an old custom, dozens of centuries old, of days and days of prayer and fasting, so that the farmers' crops would be plentiful. Everyone prayed—mothers and their children, men and boys—so that the harvest would be a happy one. In the European countries there were solemn processions through the fields by priests and people during these days.

Father records on June 10, 1900, that he is bidding farewell to the congregation. He says the salary owed him is $78.63, a debt that he leaves to the congregation to settle. He tells the parishioners that they "have a fine piece of property; that the church and house are all that need to be desired. See to it that it is kept in good repair and you will have little expense for years to come." Father was transferred to East Palestine and died December of 1900.

There is much to read about Father John Boyle so that the reader can grasp what it was like over one hundred years ago at St. Peter's under the administration of its first resident pastor.

Father Timothy O'Connell served as pastor for a short time from June 17, 1900, to July 28, 1900. He was born June 14, 1868, in Hubbardston, Michigan. Father O'Connell attended St. Francis Seminary in Milwaukee and was ordained June 24, 1894, in Milwaukee for the service of the Diocese of Grand Rapids. Before serving at St. Peter of the Fields, Father was an assistant at the Grand Rapids Cathedral, Grand Rapids, Michigan, from July 1894 until March of 1897. He then became an assistant at St. James Parish of Bay City, Michigan, where he served from March of 1897 to September of 1899. He later became the assistant pro tem at St. John Cathedral in Cleveland. He served in this capacity from January 1900 to June 17, 1900. It was at that time that he came to Rootstown. When Father O'Connell left St. Peter's, he also left the Diocese.

Father Nicholas Kirch returned to St. Peter's on August 4, 1900, and served until September 22, 1901. See Chapter II for photo since Fr. Kirch was Pastor at St. Joseph's in 1885. Father Kirch was born on October 8, 1831, in Grieweldingen, Luxemburg. He attended St. Mary Seminary in Cleveland and was ordained June 25, 1865, by Bishop Amadeus Rappe of the Cleveland Diocese. His first assignment was as Pastor at St. Mary's, Stryker. He was also asked to do missions at St. Mary's, Ederton; St. Joseph's, Florence; St. Patrick's, Bryan; St. Peter's, Archbold; and St. Caspar's, Wauseon and Springhill, from July 27, 1865, to August 21, 1867. He was next Pastor at Saints Philip and James, Canal Fulton, from August 21, 1867, to March 1875. Father Kirch served at St. Joseph's, Randolph, and St. Peter's, Rootstown, March 1875 to March 1885. He served at six other institutions from the time he left St. Joseph's and St. Peter's in March of 1885. They included serving as Pastor at St. Martin's, Liverpool (now Valley City), March 8, 1885, to October 20, 1885. He was ill from October of 1885 to May of 1886. In May of 1886 he was able to serve as Chaplain for the Humility of Mary Sisters in New Bedford, PA, until August of that year. He was Pastor at St. Barbara's, West Brookfield, September 1886 to January 1888; St. Peter's, North Ridgeville, January 8, 1888 to March 1888; St. Francis, Cleveland, March 18, 1888 to January 28, 1893; St. Clement's, Navarre, January 29, 1893 to June 22, 1893; and St. Peter's, North Ridgeville, November 12, 1893 to July 31, 1900. He was then at St. Peter's, Rootstown, until he again became ill.

He returned to service in October of 1901 as Chaplain at St. Joseph's Academy, Cleveland, until October 1902; then Chaplain at St. John's Hospital, Cleveland, until his death on February 14, 1916.

On September 20, 1901, at 12:30 PM, Father Eli Washington John Lindesmith came to St. Peter's. It is reported that he went directly to the church. He was already 74 years of age when he came to St. Peter's. Father was born September 7, 1827, in a log cabin in Columbiana County to the east in an area called Dungannon, Ohio. He was ordained by Bishop Amadeus Rappe in St. John's Cathedral, Cleveland, on July 8, 1855. Father was meticulous and kept very accurate records. His sermons were indexed and filed and are now in the archives at the Catholic University of America, Washington, D.C. Father was also very good at carpentry and made several broomsticks, candleholders, and other furniture. Some of these items are still at St. Peter's. See Chapter XI (Report Section, Report #2) for Father Lindesmith's report on the original Catholic families.

While at St. Peter's, Father spoke at the Rootstown Congregational Church about the Mass. His records indicate that he spoke "Ita Missa Est," which means "The Mass has ended, go in peace." Father's grandfather was a Revolutionary War soldier. He also had other relatives who served in the War of 1812 and the Civil War.

Father Lindesmith in his
military uniform

As evident in the following paragraphs, Father served in many areas in Northeast and North-central Ohio, at many churches and in private homes when there was no church building. After Father's ordination in 1855, he said his first Mass at St. Paul's, Dungannon. St. Paul's was the first Catholic Church in Northeast Ohio, established in 1812. Father's first assignment was pastor at St. Peter and Paul, Doylestown. This church had several missions at Canal Fulton, Marshallville, Orville, French Settlement, Clinton, North Lawrence, Millersburg, Loudonville, and Black Creek, all Father's responsibility. He also assisted as needed at Akron, Wooster, Harrisburg, Louisville, Randolph, and even far-away Mansfield. From 1858 to 1868, Father Lindesmith was assigned to St. John's, Canton, with a mission at New Berlin. On October 1, 1868, he went to Alliance. This assignment also covered the missions of Atwater, Salem, and Leetonia. (Note: Atwater is only eight miles from St. Peter's which was built in 1868 as stated earlier and where Father Lindesmith was assigned some thirty-three years later.)

In 1872, Father Lindesmith went to the Leetonia parish but retained the Salem mission and was also given the East Palestine mission. In March 1880, Bishop Richard Gilmour of the Cleveland Diocese asked Father to become a chaplain in the United States Army. In July 1880, Father was commissioned by United States President Rutherford B. Hayes as an Army Chaplain and was sent to Fort Keogh, Montana. It was during this time period that the Sioux and Sitting Bull War occurred. His military mission covered North Dakota, Wyoming, Idaho, Washington, and Oregon. During Father's time with the army, he also administered to a parish in Miles City, Montana. Father was a favorite to the army troops, and many fallen-away Catholics returned to the sacraments. His records indicate that 536 took the "abstinence from alcohol" pledge because of his influence. He was also a favorite to many non-Catholics. In 1891, at the age of sixty-five, he retired from military service.

From 1891 to 1893, Father Lindesmith was pastor of his home parish in Dungannon, where he had said his first Mass thirty-six years earlier.

In a letter dated April 23, 1904, Father Lindesmith wrote to Bishop Horstmann, of Cleveland. Father said he did not want to interfere with the people of St. Joseph and their misfortune of the loss of their church in a fire. The church had burned and there was talk of rebuilding in the town of Randolph. This new location would be two-and-a-half miles east of the present location of St. Joseph's. Father said he liked the idea of building churches in towns and near railroads as much as possible, but the Randolph location would be too close to St. Peter's, only three miles away. This would take six to ten families away from St. Peter's. Father said, "I think they would build a church at Suffield and at Rootstown Center and abandon the old St. Joseph's except for burial; this would be a good plan and what St. Peter's would lose on the west, it would gain on the east." In a letter dated April 30, 1904, the Bishop of Cleveland wrote back to Father and said that his consultants advised him that the church should be rebuilt at the old site, at St. Joseph's, since there are few families at Suffield, and most live where the old church stood.

The correspondence becomes very interesting as the reader learns later on in this book that there were <u>four such times</u> when there were thoughts and actions taken to move St. Peter's church.

In the earlier days of the church, pew rent was very important and as we have already seen in Father John Boyle's writings, pew rent was used for church expenses and the pastor's salary.

Father Lindesmith's records while he was at St. Peter's also indicate the tallying of pew rent and who paid what amount. In a 1908 financial report to the Cleveland Diocese, the total amount was $1,460.76. Father contributed $200 dollars himself. When these early financial reports are compared with the present church financial statements, it becomes quite interesting. See Chapter XI (Report Section, Report #3) for Father's financial report of 1908.

In summary, the church expense in 1908 was $1,460.76; in 1949, it was $4,000; in 1998, it was $112,097.59; in 2008 it was $271,964; and in 2009 it was $313,400.

When Father left St. Peter's in 1909 at the age of eighty-one, he became Chaplain at St. Ann's Hospital, Cleveland, serving there for thirteen years. He died February 6, 1922, at age ninety-four. He was a priest for sixty-seven years. Father Lindesmith directed his peers that there would be no sermon at his funeral; instead, Father prepared his own final homily. He instructed those who would be in charge to distribute this homily to all who came to his service. The following is the abbreviated form of Father Lindesmith's Homily. (The original was several pages longer than reported here.) These excerpts reveal much about the man and his character. They provide a fitting epitaph to this servant whose whole life was a crusade for the Lord.

Father Lindesmith's Final Homily:

We ought to think it impossible that a Christian would ever offend God: but how comes it then that Christians are so unhappy to offend him?

This comes from the malice of the enemies of our salvation, and to the negligence of the greater part of Christians, in not strengthening themselves against the snares of our spiritual enemies, by serious meditation on the truths of eternity and other holy exercises. For want of this, their faith becomes weak: and thus they become an easy prey to those enemies, and are carried away by their delusions. These enemies are the devil, the world, and the flesh.

On each of these I will make a few remarks. Our own flesh is certainly the most dangerous of the three, both because it is a domestic enemy, which we always carry about us, and it is by means of it principally, that the other two get so easily an advantage over us.

We must remember the great duty of mankind and the end for which we were created is to love, to serve and to obey God always, to study in everything to please Him, 'Whether we eat or drink, or whatever else we do, to do all for His glory.'

The whole tendency of the law of God is to restore our lost union with God and to bring back our love to Him; but the doing of this is altogether opposed to self-love. From this comes the great difficulty we find in obeying the law of God: hence those violent combats when we set ourselves in earnest to obey Him; our love of liberty can bear no restraint; and our pride to our depraved affections, and these affections blind our reason, to favor ourselves and hurry us on to actions for our own satisfaction, forgetting God and what we owe Him. The Bible calls these affections, 'The lust of the eye, the lust of the flesh, and the pride of life.'

These effects which this self-love and its lusts produce in the soul are many and dangerous. They darken the understanding, and change the judgment from truth, so as to persuade us that all these things are real goods which flatter self-love and satisfy its lusts, and that all things are evils which are contrary and disagreeable to it; they call light darkness, and darkness light; they call sweet bitter, and bitter sweet; as the word of God expresses it.

To overcome all those evils of soul and be saved, we must do three things: First, we must carefully learn all that God wants us to know; Secondly, we must heartily believe and do all that God wants of us; Thirdly, we must live a life of mortification and self denial.

The second enemy of our salvation is the world. By the world we understand that part of mankind who live in the captivity and bondage of self-love, blinded by its delusions, and slaves to its passions and concupiscence; who not only follow its suggestions, each by himself, but join, as it were, in a body, and make open profession of doing so; propagating the false principles of self-love; praising up the riches and honors, and all the pleasures and conveniences of life, as the only things worthy of our notice; esteeming and honoring them who have the greatest abundance of them; despising and understanding those who want them; and turning everything into a subject of mockery and ridicule that is contrary to their worldly opinions.

The world, then, is a disorderly crowd of various characters, who reject the principles of the gospel, have no object but their own interest; no rule for their passions; nothing gives them any concern, but what touches the riches, the pleasures, or the honors of this life.

Although the world, the enemy of the cross, takes unlimited authority, and is a tyrant over the heart of man, it is astonishing to see how it is loved, its favor sought, its frowns dreaded, even by those who in their serious thoughts are ashamed of it. It promises happiness, riches, pleasures, honors, favors of men, and everything that self-love can desire, all its maxims try to please our senses, and pet our pride, and, as we are attached to material things, we easily accept its offers. On the other hand, it threatens misery to all who reject it, holds them up to contempt, as fools who deserve to be laughed at; and as there is no kind of misery so tormenting to us as contempt, it shakes our good resolutions. Thus, 'What will the people say?' 'What will others think of me?' 'We must do as others do.' Such is the opposition we meet to a good life; therefore so many yield to the follies of the world, take a part in it, walk in its paths, turn their back to Christ, and ruin their souls.

We can see if we want to, that the whole force of those worldly notions used to draw us from our duty to God is our own fault, because we are too much attached to worldly things, for if we had not too much attachment to the pleasures of life; if we were humble of heart like our Lord; if we loved the cross of Christ, as all His servants ought to;

the world with all its evil powers could make no impression on us. We would laugh at its deceiving promises, and despise its vain threats. The remedy therefore is, learn the faith God delivered to the saints, and live up to it.

Now then, about the third enemy of our salvation, the devil, of whom the Scriptures say many things. The devil, who is the chief of the spirits of darkness, is called the prince of this world, and of him is said, 'There is no power upon the earth that can be compared with him who was made to fear no one. He beholdeth every high thing, and is king over all the children of pride.'

If it were not for our self-love, he could have no handle to attack us, nor could any of his temptations make any impressions on us, for if we neither desired those things which are flattering to self-love, nor feared what is contrary to it, it is sure neither promises of the one nor threats of the other could ever be able to move us from our duty. Therefore the best defense we can make against temptations, is to conquer our self-love by a lively faith, and self-denial as firm and constant resistance against the enemy, though his temptations should continue ever so long; never yielding, not even in small things, no matter how trifling.

For example, a drunkard to visit saloons, to keep private company with an impure person, to seek the company of infidels, and enjoy the infidel conversation and such other evil occasions, which are numerous and lead those who walk in them to wickedness and sin.

Experience teaches that those who expose themselves to the danger, fall into sin. When anything agreeable or disagreeable to us is actually present, it has a much greater force to excite our passions, for, or against it, than when it is absent; and we find it more difficult to restrain these passions in presence of the object that excites them, than when it is at a distance from us. A person moderately hungry can easily bear it; but set pleasant food before him, the sight and smell of it will so excite his appetite that it will be almost impossible not to eat. Just so, when one is in near occasion of sin by its presence, it acts so strongly upon the senses and the imagination to those sins which it offers. A man loses his money in playing cards; resolves never to play again; goes to watch others play; he soon forgets his resolution and plays again. One who got drunk, became very sorry, and made a strong resolution never to get drunk again; he visits drinking company, takes a drink or two; the next thing is that he gets drunk again. A man may be perfectly honest, but in great need of money and he has a chance to lay his hands on someone else's money—who can stand good for his honesty? Therefore the proverb: "The occasion makes a thief." How many who in decent company never think of using vulgar language, but just let them be with the vulgar and their remarks will be as obscene as any other.

For this reason, we are commanded with the strongest words to avoid evil occasions, to fly from them, both by the law of nature and the law of God.

No man must trust to the strength of his own resolution, or expose himself to the dangerous occasions, from the persuasion that he is truly determined never to be led astray by them. However strong his resolutions may be at present, when out of the occasion, what security can he have that he will not be overcome by its presence? Is he stronger than Samson, more pious than David, wiser than Solomon, or more faithful than Peter? They fell by being exposed to the occasion; what can he expect?

Do not say, 'I trust in God, who will keep me from harm,' and then willfully expose yourself. God certainly will protect us when we are exposed in the line of our duty, or when Providence permits us to be in danger (but) we have no reason or promise to expect such protection when we willfully expose ourselves to danger without a good reason.

Such pretended confidence in God is tempting to God; it is highly sinful; it is transgressing His command, which orders us to remain away from the danger.

In conclusion, remember the principal means God gives us to overcome enemies of our salvation are included under the following heads: First, we must carefully learn all that God wants us to know. Secondly, we must with a good will believe all that God wants us to believe. Thirdly, we must do what God wants us to do. Fourthly, we must refrain from doing what God tells us not to do. Fifthly, we must live a life of mortification and self-denial. Having lived such a life, we will be able at our death to say with St. Paul: "I have fought the good fight, I have finished the course, I have kept the faith."

In my dying hour I wish you all this blessing: In the name of the Father, and of the Son and of the Holy Ghost. Amen.

Several books, volumes, and files are housed in the archives of Catholic University of America, Washington, D.C. A notable action that Father Lindesmith took was to set up grants at the university for those studying for the priesthood.

Father Lindesmith wrote about many incidents in his life even as a young man. Once, after a switching he received in school because of a mistaken identity, he wrote, "Never punish a child without a full investigation. And if you are unjustly punished don't be too much astonished; for millions of good people have been unjustly punished; among them eleven of the twelve apostles, and Jesus Christ our redeemer and savior."

Father John P. McGoogan served at St. Peter's from 1909 to 1919. He was an Irish priest and an accomplished musician. He formed a church band but had no suitable place to practice, so he had the church basement dug out. This excavation was accomplished by horses, mules, and slip scrapers. One team was owned by Henry C. Kline who lived directly across the road from the church. Another team was owned by Clarence Kline, father of former parishioner John Kenneth Kline, now deceased who lived one mile north of the church on Kline Road. The team of mules was owned by Ernie Paulus, a farmer down by Johnny Cake Hollow to the south of the church.

Fr. McGoogan
1909 ~ 1919

Three Kline brothers—Clarence on the clarinet and piano, Cornelous on the violin, and Cletus on the trombone—played in Father McGoogan's band. Another parishioner, Urban Knapp, played drums. Father McGoogan played violin.

Father was a fun-loving person, and once when returning to the parish at night, he ran his car over the bank west of the church and down into the creek. He was pulled out by two teams of horses. A long time parishioner reported that Father imbibed occasionally.

Apparently Father was not very happy at St. Peter's. In a letter dated October 12, 1918, sent to the Bishop, Father says "I've been here for nine years, and I hope you haven't forgot [sic] me. Sometimes I think you have."

Many dances and socials were held in the church basement and grounds in the early 1900s. The basement was also used for plays. The church had a club named "Royal Club of St. Peter's Catholic Church." Once they put on a three-act play called *There's a Man in The House*. *Abbey's Irish Rose* was another play. The play director at that time was Father Walter Fowler who came in the 1930s.

In 1919, Father Louis A. LeMiller came from Stark County. He was ordained in New Orleans as a missionary priest. He would politely grill the Sunday school children as he paced back and forth: How many minutes in an hour? How many weeks in a year? Who is God? Why did God make you? He was known as a very pleasant and easy-going person. He returned to the missions out West in 1923.

The archives at Kent State University contain a report from Father LeMiller to Chancellor Rev. P.J.O. O'Connell, dated May 31, 1923, where Father sent thirteen dollars to the Diocese for the Seminary Collection. This money came from the thirteen following identified parishioners: John Marquart, John Bart, William Englehart, John Winkler, Albert Mitsch, George Klein, Henry Kline, John Albinger, William Schroeder, Mrs. Henry Luli, George Hostler, Oliver Knapp, and Louisa Knapp.

A January 19, 1923, letter from the Chancellor authorized Mass to be said twice a month at New Milford. Since no official records could be found, it is not known if the Masses actually took place.

Anthony Battes
1923 - 1927

Father Anthony A. Battes served St. Peter's from 1923 to 1927. He was a German priest educated in Herschbach, Germany; attended Bishop's College in Monta Bur, Germany; and graduated from the seminary in Fulda, Germany. He was known as a very strict priest and, according to my uncle Lawrence Winkler, would pull the ear or cheek of youngsters if they didn't know their Catechism. Uncle Lawrence was a young lad at St. Peter's at this time.

Father Battes had to live with parishioners for a time because the parish house had been neglected for so long and had to be repaired. It was during this time that some of St. Peter's parishioners helped build the Lourdes Grotto at St. Joseph's as mentioned in Chapter II. Another interesting bit of information shared with the author by Uncle Lawrence was that parishioners could park their horses and buggies across the road under a shed at the Henry C. Kline farm and that there was a bucket hanging on a post for donations. When asked what a parishioner would put in the bucket, he said probably a nickel.

Father Siegfried W. Heyl, S.T.D., then served from 1927 to 1933. He was ordained in Innsbruck, Germany, in 1911. The population of the church had dropped considerably during these years. Father Heyl had a German accent and drove a large car (reportedly a 4-door

Studebaker with solid steel rims). Eloise (Sweet) Biltz, long-time parishioner, reported that she had received her First Holy Communion under Father Heyl. She said there were only four, three girls and one boy, in the class. See Chapter XI (Report Section, Report #5) for more information from the interview and report of Eloise (Sweet) Biltz.

The housekeeper for Father Heyl, Mrs. Lais, had a very pretty daughter. Parishioner Lawrence Winkler had a date with her, but when he asked for a second date, Father Heyl said, "You'd better not take her out again; she's too young."

Father Fowler was made pastor of the Rootstown parish September 7, 1933. Father Fowler was born June 2, 1898, in Cleveland, the son of Mrs. Rose and the late John Fowler. He

Fr. Walter Fowler
1933 - 1941

attended St. Patrick's School, Bridge Avenue, and St. Ignatius High School and College. He studied theology at St. Bernard's Seminary, Rochester, NY. He was ordained by Archbishop Joseph Schrembs on February 24, 1923, in St. John's Cathedral, and his first assignment was as an assistant at the St Aloysius Parish, East Liverpool. Three years later, in 1926, he was make assistant at Our Lady of Peace Parish, Cleveland, and a few months later at St. Joseph's Parish, Collinwood. Because of illness, Father Fowler was given a leave of absence for two years. He served as assistant at St. Edward's Parish, September 12, 1928, to April 26, 1929, when he was made assistant at St. Gregory's Parish, South Euclid, Ohio.

While at St. Peter's, Father Fowler was asked to give the commencement address at Rootstown School. His remarks were well received, and he was afforded a standing ovation. The town folks talked about his address for years.

The Reidinger farm next door to the east of the church was purchased during this time. Paul Reidinger who still lived in the farm house rang the church bell at 6 AM, 12 Noon, and 6 PM. The parishioners at home and in the fields would hear the bell and say the Angeles Prayer.

Parishioners Louis Biltz, Rupert Strickland, and Ernie Paulus took Father Fowler around to several fallen away Catholic families. The church grew from 18 families to 67 in a few years because of these visits. There had been much fighting between Germans and Italians, and Father Fowler smoothed things out. It was found that some didn't like the hard cider and sauerkraut smell of the Germans, and some didn't like the wine and garlic smell of the Italians in church. It was also reported that all but three of these families had farms.

The large crucifix at the north end of the cemetery was put in place with plans to build an outdoor altar for special Masses. This altar was completed by Father Delmege who followed Father Fowler as Pastor. A tribute to the Fowler family was engraved on the front of this altar.

Many chicken dinners were held in the church basement and people came from Akron and Cleveland. Plays continued to be held and were directed by Father Fowler. Feather parties were held in the fall. Feather parties consisted of playing Bingo with a turkey as the prize. Bingo was very popular and parishioner John Rodenbucher supplied many free turkeys from his turkey farm on Lansinger Road, now called Old Forge Road.

Father was responsible for having Catholic children excused from Rootstown Public School on Holy Thursday and Good Friday. Lawrence Winkler said he took Father to many basketball games. One such game was between the Atwater Redmen (all farm boys) and the Ravenna Knights of Columbus. The Knights were badly beaten. Lawrence also related how he would accompany Father on trips to the I.R. Root Co., Medina, to purchase church candles. At one time, Father Fowler had a new Dodge automobile. Lawrence said Father just loved to drive it. This beloved priest died January 22, 1941, in St. Thomas Hospital, Akron, Ohio, and was buried at his request near the cross that he had erected in St. Peter's cemetery. Father's grave is located at the extreme north end of the cemetery, a few feet south of the cross.

Father Fowler's housekeeper was Catherine Wohlwend Orgwally from Suffield, Ohio. She was married to Mr. Martin Knipp from Alliance, Ohio. An interview with Mr. Martin Knipp became very interesting because of his connection to St. Peter's as an altar boy in the 1920s and bell ringer for the Angeles prayer. His interview can be found in Chapter XI (Report Section, Report #4).

Father Robert D. Delmege born on December 5, 1897, was assigned as administrator in 1940 because of Father Fowler's poor health. Father Delmege became pastor June 29, 1941, coming from Cleveland. He was ordained April 2, 1929, and had served at several churches in Cleveland. He was a WWI veteran. Father Delmege had considerable experience in accounting as he had worked for a large nationally-known manufacturing firm in Cleveland before his priesthood.

Upon first arriving at St. Peter's, Father Delmege requested the Diocese to authorize him to stay in the Ravenna Hotel for a time while the parish house was being renovated as it had been quite run-down.

St. Peter's had forty families when Father arrived. He had the parish renamed St. Peter of the Fields to distinguish it from other St. Peter's in the diocese. In this same year, he had an office built on the front of the rectory, basically by having the front porch enclosed. In 1942, the front and rear of the church had additions put on and the exterior and interior of the church were painted. In 1947, the church and rectory were remodeled. The church was actually remodeled May to July 1947. It is interesting to note that the parish was known as St. Peter's for 73 years, 1868 to 1941, and known as St. Peter of the Fields for 69 years, from 1941 to the present, 2010.

Father Delmege kept the parish informed about parish veterans serving in WW II. In the July 1943 parish bulletin, Father listed the names of those serving in the Great War. See Chapter XI (Report Section, Report #6) for a copy of that bulletin.

The following is a letter written to Father by veteran Paul Knapp. It was found in the *Gleaning*, the church paper, of June 3, 1945.

Dear Father,

Well, I am writing from India! Since we left the States we have been very busy after a long trip across the ocean. I am not only a long way from Rootstown but I'm on the other side of the world—imagine! Though it does seem queer to be so far from home going to Mass every Sunday—the very same Mass in Rootstown!—I pray that He will bring me back home safely.

For a soldier I am occupied with a very unsoldierly occupation but it is work that must be done over here; namely, I am working on making drums in a very modern factory; drums for the gas that is flown over 'the hump' to China. Though we are not in the front lines we can expect a bit of bombing any time. But speaking of work again the natives really do the work; we merely show them how. These natives are certainly poor and they have hardly enough to eat. Thanks to the good God that I was born a native of the good old USA! It gives me a heart ache to see the squalor in which the little children must live and how little there is in life for any of them.

While the weather is fine it is very hot and the natives are preparing against the monsoon season by getting the rice fields ready.

Of course all of us want to come home and I hope the people of St. Peter's will continue to pray that this eastern war will soon end and let us return to normal life and living.

Private Jack Leyland, born October 5, 1922, was the only soldier killed in World War II from the parish. Jack served with the 504 Parachute Infantry Regiment of the 82nd Airborne Division. He was killed January 25, 1944, on Anzio Beach, Italy. Jack is buried in the Sicily Rome-American Cemetery and Memorial, thirty miles south of Rome in the town of Nettuno. His plot is H, row 14, grave 1. There is a memorial stone marker for him beside his parents' graves in St. Peter's Cemetery.

On May 30, 2010, a special memorial service was held at Private Leyland's memorial marker by Pastor Father David Misbrenner, the parish Catholic War Veterans, and members of the 82nd Airborne Division Association, Akron Chapter's Honor Guard.

Under the direction of Father Delmege, the cemetery at St. Peter's was a showplace with flowering bushes of white spirea. Father would ask the parishioners to save some of their seeds in the fall and give them to him for the cemetery. A driveway on the west side of the church was improved and lined with sandstone. A large twelve-foot iron gate was installed behind the church to serve as the entrance to the cemetery. This was done so funeral hearses could enter the cemetery from the west side. A small swinging pedestrian gate was installed immediately next to the large gate. The author recalls very clearly Father showing off this swinging gate. He pointed out that the gate opened both ways. He was so proud of it. See Chapter XI (Photo Section, Photos #18-#20) for cemetery and cemetery entrance.

Father Delmege was determined to have parishioners follow his request for church participation during Mass and all religious services. He stated in a church bulletin dated 25 February 1945 in heavy print: *"Sunday School for children is useless unless you help them during the week."* Forty- Hours' Devotion was a well-attended service both by parishioners and visiting priests. The author, as a young lad of about ten, remembers the many priests who came for 40 Hours' Devotion. Paul Reidinger who lived next door to the church in the farm house said they were loud and played cards into the wee-hours of the morning.

Once, as a young lad, the author was asked by Father to weed the flowers planted around the foundation of the parish house. This author did just as asked, pulling up all the weeds <u>and</u> all the flowers. Father just stood there and looked without saying a word. At least not out loud.

Another time this author was serving Mass, again as a young lad, and had a runny nose. Father handed him a handkerchief. This altar boy blew his nose and then attempted to hand the handkerchief back to Father. Father Delmege abruptly exclaimed, "Take it home and wash it!" He would also ask the altar boys how tall they were and how much they weighed. Indeed, Father inspected the altar boys for clean fingernails and shined shoes as well.

Father Delmege purchased, with his own money, the life-size statue of Christ in the cemetery and the life-size statue of St. Peter which originally stood on the west side of the church. The statue of St. Peter has now been moved to a position between the historic church and the new church. St. Peter and St. Anthony statues inside the church were also purchased by him. See Chapter XI (Photo Section, Photos #50 & #51) to view these statues.

Father Delmege assisted men of the parish in completing the large stone altar at the back or north end of the cemetery. This altar, including the large crucifix, was paid for by the family of Father Fowler.

On October 23, 1943, Father advised the then Bishop McFadden that the church floor supports were replaced since there was grave danger of the entire floor collapsing. Bishop Hoban had advised Father in an earlier visit to St. Peter's that the church should be located at Rootstown center and to make only necessary repairs to the church. Bishop McFadden who succeeded Bishop Hoban advised Father to make all repairs permanent and begin the remodeling of the church as there was no need at present time to move the church and lose its beautiful rural setting and memories. Later, Father Delmege advised the bishop that a stand of timber had been purchased by a contractor and was being cleared, sawed, kiln dried, and milled for the church renovation. See Chapter XI (Letter Section, Letter #1) for Father Delmege's request and Bishop McFadden's reply.

Father Delmege reminded everyone in a church bulletin dated June 3, 1945, that the Infant of Prague statue in the church was brought to St. Peter's by the first resident pastor Father John Boyle and that it was touched to the original statue in Prague, Czechoslovakia. This information was more fully developed as we read earlier under Father Boyle's time as first resident pastor.

In 1945, Father Delmege published a letter and a chart on what he expected of his parishioners. See Chapter XI (Chart Section, Chart #2 followed by a letter of explanation).

A metal bee-hive type tabernacle was purchased and installed by a friend of Father Delmege. A single family donated the money for the communion railing. New pews were installed and half of the cost was paid for by Mrs. Albert Jacobs (Cora Kline) of Kent, Ohio. Mrs. Jacobs was long-time parishioner William Kline's sister and aunt of present-day parishioner Henry J. Kline. A check for $2000 was enclosed in a letter from the diocesan chancellor, Alford J. Heinrich, on August 21, 1946. Father Delmege personally borrowed $1000 to add to the bishop's loan for remodeling. A report went back to the chancellor on January 3, 1949, stating that all loans were now paid in full.

When long-time parishioner and farmer Ernest Paulus passed away, Father said, "He was ready. Are you ready?" This author personally heard this comment. Born in 1887, Ernie was the second oldest of seven children of the Paulus family from Johnny Cake Hollow. His siblings— Gertrude born in 1884; Grace, 1891; Albert, 1893; Edward and Mary, 1898; and Clarence, 1901—all worked on the Paulus farm and attended daily Mass many times at St. Peter's. The barn and house still stand on Johnny Cake Road. This family is mentioned here because they were among the early pillars of the church.

Stray Hogs Ruin Cemetery Grounds

During Father's time at St. Peter's, he reported a very interesting happening in the cemetery, which the local newspaper also reported: A farmer's hogs had gotten loose and "ruined" the church cemetery.

In 1954 after much planning, repairing, and building at St. Peter's and thirteen years service there, Father Delmege was transferred to a parish in Louisville, Ohio. He became chaplain of the Louisville Knights of Columbus and the Louisville American Legion. Soon, he became a Monsignor and was appointed Domestic Prelate by Pope John XXIII in 1961. Father retired on July 15, 1967, and moved to Florida, taking with him his long-time housekeeper from St. Peter's and St. Louis, Thelma Biltz of Rootstown. Father was a priest for thirty-eight years. He wrote a brief history of his beloved St. Peter's. See Chapter XI (Document Section, Document #6) for a history report by Father Delmege. Even though this book contains the information found therein, Father's report is included because it is Father's own original work found in the Church's archives.

The church's *Gleaning* Sunday publication of July 24, 1949, reported that the parish monthly expense was $325. Contrast that with today's weekly expenses of approximately $4,000.

Father Joseph Tomasch came to St. Peter's in 1954. He was ordained April 2, 1938, by Bishop Schremes, Cleveland. Father had attended St. Boniface and St. Ignatius, Cleveland, Ohio, and John Carroll and St. Mary's Seminary. When he was at St. Peter's, his mother was his

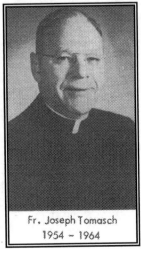

Fr. Joseph Tomasch
1954 – 1964

37

housekeeper. One of the first major accomplishments by Father was to purchase the Reidinger farm adjoining church property immediately to the east. He formed St. Peter's Co-op group to assist the farmers. He had the Reidinger house remodeled and rented out. Parishioner James Winkler and others did the work. One of the renters was the Moneypenny family, and parishioner Helen Winkler Parry babysat for them in the Reidinger house.

A new Hammond organ was purchased for the church. Bingo became popular again to help with parish expenses. The Knights of Columbus and the CYO (Catholic Youth Organization) were established. Parishioner Stanley Ambrose was the first Grand Knight for the Knights of Columbus, Rootstown Council. Stanley said he wasn't exactly "elected"; Father simply told him, "You will be our first Grand Knight."

Trudy Winkler Shrigley, Rose Winkler Darling, Helen Winkler Parry, Christine Kline Luli, Joan and Marie Rice, and many other young adults decorated the old barn. Linda Kline Easterday, Christine's sister, also was active with the youth group as were Ronald Knapp, William Kline, Larry Kline, Ray Luli, Charles Miley, Bob Hillgart, Kenneth Adelman, Jim, Jeff and Jane Gishnock, and Tess Motz. A stage was erected in the barn and the CYO held many dances there. Square dance and other types of dance lessons were given. The Joe Esposito Band provided the music. Youth from the surrounding area would stand on the barn hill waiting to get in as it was a very popular place to go. See Chapter XI (Report Section, Report #7) from Joan and Marie Rice.

Spaghetti dinners were cooked in a small kitchen in the basement of the historic church and served there by the youth. Due to the illness of Father Tomasch, Bishop Walsh of Youngstown appointed Father Albert E. Meyer as assistant in September of 1957. Father Albert was a giant of a man. He loved to travel to the Winkler farm for homemade bread and cookies. Sometimes he drove around in his open Jeep in winter time with no side curtains.

Father assisted Father Tomasch especially with the youth groups. He organized dance parties at the Reidinger barn. He also organized ice skating parties at the Rita and Roy Cline pond on State Route 44 south of Rootstown Center. Rita and Roy were the parents of Christine Cline Luli. Father Albert was also a very good photographer and, in fact, took the photos at this author's wedding in 1958.

Sometime after Father Meyer left St. Peter's, he sent a letter to the Winkler family dated April 9, 1960. He explained that he was in Mexico assisting with a new seminary in Morelia near Mexico City; there was a severe shortage of priests there. He said there were 5,000 Catholics to each priest. Father ended his letter by saying, "It is still against the law to be a priest in Mexico, so my name there is Albert Meyer, not Father Albert Meyer." Many times Father found it necessary to carry a gun.

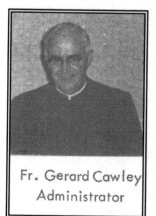

Fr. Gerard Cawley
Administrator

Fr. Patrick Conway s.P.
Sunday Assistant

Father Patrick Conway, S.P., also assisted at St. Peter's from 1950 to 1970. Father Conway's main duties were to assist as needed on Sundays, again because of the illness of Father Joseph Tomasch.

In 1958, Father Gerald Cawley came and served as administrator until 1959. Father Cawley was instrumental in the building of the church hall and supervised this project because Father Tomasch was in very poor health. Father Cawley issued a letter on August 18, 1959, to all parishioners that he desired 100% participation for work and finances on the new hall. The hall construction started in the fall of 1959 and was completed in the summer of 1960. See Chapter XI (Letter Section, Letter #3) for this correspondence.

It is simply amazing how this hall was built and by whom. Parishioner George Luli Sr. was the construction boss. P.L. Frank, owner of P.L. Frank Construction Co., Ravenna, Ohio, supplied much of the material and allowed his workers to build the hall while on his payroll. Many parishioners also donated their time. See Chapter XI (Photo Section, Photo #25) for a photo of the groundbreaking including names of parishioners involved.

Mr. Glen Christ was the masonry foreman. George, Charles, and Kenny Bildershine and Philmore Smith dug the septic system ditch back to the septic tank east of the hall by hand.

Oscar Horning and John Kline of Horning's Construction, Randolph, excavated and poured the hall floor. Morgan Dockerty, a tall, rugged man put on the roof. Ray, George, and John Luli, sons of George Luli Sr. worked as carpenters. Bill Luli, another son of George Sr., John Rodenbucher (turkey farmer), and John Drego from Drego Plumbing, Ravenna, did the plumbing. Bill Anthony did the electrical work. Sidney Knapp made the kitchen cabinets. John Adams and Ray Luli did the beautiful brick work at the hall entrance. A large steel cross, twenty feet high, was built into the brick wall.

Dedication of the new hall was on June 18, 1960. There were 375 attendees. Bishop Walsh was a guest. Music was provided by the Louis Esposito Band, along with Robert Burns, John L. Winkler (father of the author), Kenny Kline, and Rupert Strickling.

Father Patrick Gallagher served from 1960 to 1962 for a thirteen-month period. Father Gallagher worked to upgrade the altar-boys' role in the church. Father also added a third Mass on Sundays. Several guilds were also started or renewed at this time. See Chapter IV for a list of guilds and sodalities.

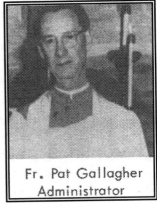

Fr. Pat Gallagher
Administrator

Father Thomas McNally then served from 1963 to 1964, a nine month period. Several priests served from 1954 to 1964 as mentioned earlier because of the failing health of Father Tomasch.

Fr. Thomas McNally
Administrator

Father Allen Simpson came on January 17, 1964, and served until his untimely death in July of 1968. He was a native of Ottumwa, Iowa, and was ordained on February 2, 1948, at St. Columba, Youngstown, Ohio. When Father Simpson was ordained a Catholic priest, he was one of only twenty-eight black priests in the entire United States. Father said his first Mass on February 8, 1948, at Conception, Missouri. Father had been a counselor for Father Flanagan at Boys' Town during the summer of 1948, so Father Flanagan preached the sermon at Father's first Mass.

Father Simpson was the grandson of a Methodist minister and one of nine children. After his own conversion to the Catholic faith, his mother and eight brothers and sisters joined the Catholic Church as well.

Fr. Allen M. Simpson
1964 -

Father's first assignment was at St. Patrick's of Kent, Ohio, where he served from 1948 to 1964. During Father's time at St. Peter's, he had the Reidinger house removed. As mentioned earlier, this was the youth group meeting place in the 1950s and early 1960s, but it was no longer needed because the new hall was built in 1960. A picnic area and ball field were built behind the cemetery by the Rootstown Knights of Columbus. Numerous ball games and picnics occurred there in those years.

Soundproof and fire-proof curtains were installed in the new church hall for CCD. Father worked intensely on updating the Mass liturgy and increasing parishioner participation. He was a very popular priest, humble and sincere. The church was so full at Masses that people stood along the outside aisles from the rear to the front of the church.

In 1968, Father Simpson announced a three day, 100 year centennial celebration at St. Peter's. There were several parishioners on the planning committee. See Chapter XI (Photo Section, Photos #26 &#27) for planning committee and Centennial dinner.

Father Simpson was involved in other activities outside of his assignment at St. Peter's. He was the Diocesan moderator for the Infant of Prague Guild and a speaker at interracial church conferences.

The church bulletin, *Gleanings*, was issued each Sunday and usually had challenging statements or explanatory statements at the bottom. One such statement, dated July 16, 1967, read: "A great many so-called open minds should be closed for repairs." Another dated January 7, 1968, offered this insight: "Treasures in Heaven are laid up only as treasures on Earth are laid down." Father Simpson was interested in the science of palm reading and while attending a conference on such topics in Chicago in 1968, Father passed away.

An interesting question was asked of Father Simpson, and he put the question and answer in the church *Gleanings* dated July 9, 1967:

"Question: I saw a picture of a whole parish receiving Communion under the form of bread and wine. Since many Communicants were young, would this perhaps not start a habit of alcoholism for some? What about infection from drinking of the same cup? Answer: Wine dispensed in Communion is very small in quantity. Any habit of alcoholism would arise quite apart from such an experience. We have never heard of a single case of disease communicated by wine dispensed in Communion. Were there such a case, the practice would be stopped where it occurred."

Father Michael Gawron served St. Peter's from 1968 to 1981. He was ordained June 29, 1936, in Tarnow, Poland. He attended school in Gostyn, Poland, and came to the United States in 1953. Father was a POW (prisoner of war) in a Nazi concentration camp. He said that at one time he weighed eighty pounds while in prison.

Many times during his sermons, he would touch the fire of the burning candle and talk about the "Light of the World" Jesus Christ.

During Father's time at St. Peter's, he had the church and the Stations of the Cross repainted and the church aisles re-carpeted.

The life-size crucifix at the very front of the Church was carved by a man, name unknown, from Atwater, Ohio, around 1900. The painting on the front wall of the Holy Land was originally provided by Father Robert Delmege and was displayed there from 1950 to 1968. It represents the Holy Trinity: the Father, Son and Holy Spirit. When the church was painted during Father Allen Simpson's time, it was painted over. In the spring of 1978, Father Michael Gawron commissioned Mary Raynesdal Kline, daughter of John Kenneth and Rose Kline, to paint a reproduction of the original. Father Gawron had slides and photographs of the original. Father had an 8" x10" picture made from the slides and photo, and Mary Kline painted the present picture. It is painted on a large sheet of Masonite so that it can be removed. See Mary Kline Raynesdal's Report regarding her work in Chapter XI (Report Section, Report #8).

Father Gawron knew detailed information about each family, their children and their work. He also would correspond with those serving in the Armed Forces. When he retired, he moved to Alliance, Ohio. He was a priest for forty years. He said to this author one time, "How is the policeman?" I was rather surprised because I had no idea that he knew I was an Ohio State patrolman for several years.

Father was a strict priest, especially regarding babies crying in church or parishioners wearing improper clothing (shorts) to Mass or talking instead of praying before Mass. He would tell people specifically not to wear shorts and other leisurely type clothing to Mass.

In 1976 there was a big celebration in the church hall. Father's priest friends Father Leo Dobosiewicz from St. Joseph's, Campbell, Ohio, and Monsignor Robert Brengartner St. Patrick's Kent, Ohio, were present. Father Brengartner was a former Navy chaplain.

Father Gawron had to retire in 1981 because of his age; he was 75 years old. Upon his retirement, he had made nearly $500,000 for the parish by saving and by an intelligent investment strategy.

Rev. John Sargent
Pastor

Father John Sargent came to St. Peter's on July 1, 1981, and served until his retirement in 1995. However, he did not retire completely as he assisted Father Kevin Fete at the Church of The Little Flower, Hartville, Ohio. Father came from Canton where he had been pastor at a much larger St. Peter's and the Catholic school there for several years. Under Father's direction, fish dinners during Lent became very popular county-wide. Sauerkraut dinners were held in the fall including a harvest festival with crafts for sale. An active parish council was developed and improvements were made to the rectory by enlarging rooms and adding a new kitchen. An attached garage was constructed for Father's car and motorcycle and maintenance equipment. The historic church basement was renovated with small rooms for classes and meetings. Air conditioning was added to the church and special cover windows were installed to protect the beautiful historic stained glass windows of the church. These historic windows bear the donors' names of years ago.

During this time, the church hall kitchen and bathrooms were updated mostly under the direction of former parishioner, Vernon Clapp. Parishoners who worked on the project were as follows: Roy Paulus, Kenneth Kline, Steven Kline, Jim Winkler, the Charles Miley family, Jerry Meloy, John Duffy, Larry Bresky, Bob Cook, Elmer Riemenschneider, Scott Riemenschneider, Stanley Ambrose, Richard Hendershot, George Bildershine, Steve Paulus, Scott Krieger, Paul Krieger, Greg Krieger, Jim Albright, Ron Albright, Ron Feciuch, Dave Moledor, Jerry Meadows, Lee Jenior, Randy Bradly, Bill Householder, Robert Walker, Ray Luli, Lenard Winlin, Sandy Pettigrew, Gordon Tomko, Frank Fleckstiner, Harry Rorer, Jerry King, Phil Smith, Kenny Smith, Walter Laskos, David Jakubisin, Charles Angle, and Jim Testa. Certain other parishioners and non-parishioners whose names could not be identified also assisted with this project.

Priests that served as assistants during these years came from the Blessed Sacrament Fathers, Canton, Ohio; Brunnerdale Seminary, Cleveland; Catholic Central, Canton; and The Society of Saint Paul, Canfield, Ohio. They were Fathers Deffenbaugh, Chenevey, Fogarty and Rothrig.

On September 26, 1993, a 125 year anniversary celebration was held. The hall was filled with dinner guests. Lawrence Winkler, mentioned earlier, said the "Our Father" in German. Lauris MacEwen, council president, and her son Jack did the catering. Judy Hendershot provided the music for singing. Eloise Biltz Sweet paid tribute to the church's many pastors. Former parishioner David Moulton was the master of ceremonies. David was a teacher at Maplewood Vocational School and also a CCD teacher at St. Peter's. A special celebration Mass was held and the church was packed with people standing along the sides of the church down to the altar. Videos were made of this Mass and celebration. See Chapter XI (Photo Section, Photo #28) for a photo of the celebration dinner.

Father Sargent loved to ride his motorcycle, and he would often times drive it to the New Milford Post Office to pick up his mail. Once he had a rather serious accident on the highway with his bike. In later years, after retirement, he was trying to move his motorcycle and it fell on him and broke his ankle.

Few people were aware that Father Sargent was an accomplished pianist and he loved classical music. Monsignor Robert Sabatino, from the Immaculate Conception Church, Ravenna, Ohio, now retired, once told this author that he went to see Father Sargent, and as he walked up to the rectory, he heard beautiful piano music. When he rang the doorbell, the music abruptly stopped. Father came to the door, but not a word was mentioned about music. A stray cat came to the parish house at St. Peter's, and Father took it in. They became friends for life. Father Sargent said once from the pulpit that St. Peter's was the most relaxing parish he had ever been assigned to.

As stated in Chapter II, Deacon Tom Shay was originally assigned to St. Joseph's, Randolph, Ohio, in 1991. In 1992, Deacon Shay was assigned to St. Peter's to assist Father Sargent. Deacon Thomas Shay was born in Braddock, PA, on May 26, 1928. He graduated from Braddock High School May 25, 1945, and enlisted in the US Army on September 6, 1946. He was honorably discharged on January 8, 1947, due to the death of his father. He then went on to receive a Bachelor of Arts and Science degree from Duquesne University in 1950 where he studied philosophy, marketing, and public speaking. He also graduated from the University of Pittsburgh in 1967 with a Bachelor of Science degree in pharmacy. He worked as a district supervisor at a Revco Drug chain in eastern Ohio and western Pennsylvania. He is married to Sherry Y. Shay with whom he has nine children, fourteen grandchildren, and three great-grandchildren. Deacon Shay received his training for the deaconate through the Diocese of Youngstown by panels of priests. He was ordained December 14, 1991, and then served at St. Joseph's church in Randolph. He returned to St. Peter of the Fields on the First Sunday of Advent of 1992.

Deacon Tom Shay

Deacon Shay took a suggestion from the parish council and made contact with the Diocese of Youngstown for information to establish a sister church. It was learned that Jim Dorin from Youngstown had been staying at a church called Queen of All Saints in Beattyville, Kentucky, on a volunteer basis to assess the building needs of that community. It was reported by Deacon Shay that the church could benefit in many ways from St. Peter's support. Deacon Shay traveled to Queen of All Saints and met with Sister Davida Lund, Pastoral Associate of the parish. Deacon Shay was advised that what the people really needed was clothing.

Barbara Kline, parishioner at St. Peter's, became the coordinator of the Beattyville Committee and served in that capacity for seven years from 1994 to 2001. One time, Barbara's son Stephen took a semi-truck-load of goods to Beattyville from St. Peter's.

The priest at Queen of All Saints was Father Richard Edelen. His assignment was that of pastor of three other area churches besides Queen of All Saints. He had to travel the hills of Kentucky constantly to accomplish all his duties.

In 1995, Sister Alice Retzner became the Pastoral Associate of Queen of All Saints. In 1998, donations from St. Peter's, Rootstown, and St. Joseph's, North Bend, Cincinnati, Ohio, made it possible for a new storage building at Queen of All Saints. An auto was also purchased for Father Edelen as his much-used car had 190,000 miles on it.

In 1996, Sisters Davida and Alice visited St. Peter's and reported to the parishioners on the progress of their church. The present pastor at Beattyville, Kentucky, is Father Mike Weglicki who has been there since 2005.

The St. Peter's Beattyville Committee is an on-going project at this writing (2010), coordinated by the Church's Altar Rosary Society.

Father Terrance Hazel came to St. Peter's as Canonical Pastor on 18 August 1995 and served until February 10, 1997. He was born May 21, 1949, and was ordained June 7, 1975, at St. Columba, Youngstown, by Bishop Malone. He had a B.A. in philosophy from St. Gregory's Seminary, a Masters in Theology from Mount St. Mary's Seminary, Cincinnati, and a Masters in Education from Ursuline College, Cleveland. Upon leaving St. Peter's, he was assigned to St. Michael's, Canfield.

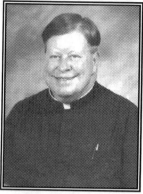

Father Hazel had a long and impressive list of assignments prior to coming to St. Peter's: He was Pro-Tem Assistant at St. Edward's Parish, Youngstown; was on the faculty at Ursuline High School; was Director of Ministry to the deaf for Mahoning and Trumbull Counties; was Administrative Assistant for Pastoral Ministry at John F. Kennedy High School, Warren; then associate principal at that school until 1986; then appointed principal at St. Thomas Aquinas H.S., Louisville. He also served on the Youngstown Diocesan Priests' Senate, the Diocesan Board of Religious Education, and was the Diocesan Coordinator of Religious Education for the mentally retarded.

In 1995, Sister Regina Zeleznik from the Sisters of Notre Dame Provincial Center, Chardon, Ohio, was assigned to St. Peter's parish as Administrator. She served in that capacity until August 13, 1999. Sister Regina had served twenty-two years as principal in Youngstown and Cleveland schools. She had taught eleven years in Youngstown, Cleveland, and Virginia. She had also done pastoral work in Raleigh, North Carolina. Early in her career, Sister taught catechism classes at St. Joseph's, Randolph. One of her first grade students was Christine Ambrose, daughter of St. Peter's parishioners Stanley and Caroline Ambrose and niece of Helen Ambrose Gless. Mrs. Gless was principal of the St. Peter's religious program for many years. Her career is covered in chapter VI.

Sister Regina Zeleznik

Sister Regina began a movement at the parish of St. Peter's to build more worship space. With the services of a Cleveland architect firm (Tomsic and Tomsic), Sister had three schemes or

plans printed up to provide for more space. One was to add on to the existing church; another was to extend in an L shape from the existing church to the hall; and the third was to build east of the present church and rectory. None of these plans materialized for several reasons. There was lack of support from certain parishioners, lack of clearly defined requirements from the Environmental Protection Agency (EPA) for a septic system, and a slow response from the Portage County Building Department. Sister Regina left the parish in 1999 and returned to the Provincial Center in Chardon, Ohio. Sister Regina died June 13, 2007.

Father Patrick Manning was assigned as Canonical Pastor to St. Peter's from February 10, 1997 to April 27, 1998. He was born in Center City, Youngstown, Ohio, and was ordained in July of 1978 at St. Mary's Seminary, Cincinnati, Ohio. He studied for four years at the Vatican. He taught at St. Thomas Aquinas High School, Louisville, Ohio, at J.F.K. High School, Warren, and part-time at Hiram and Walsh Colleges.

Father Manning was a colorful priest with a neck and shoulders like a weight-lifter. He said one time in his sermon that his seminary superiors told him he wasn't smart enough to be a priest and now he has four degrees, has studied in Rome, and has met the Pope. He was well liked by all, and the parishioners hoped that he would stay at St. Peter's. As he stated many times, this was his wish too.

Father Paul Gubser served as Sacramental Minister from July 4, 1998 to March 22, 1999. Father Paul was not well and had to leave the parish after nine months.

Father Frederick Trucksis served at St. Peter's from March 27, 1999 to August 13, 1999 as Sacramental Minister. He gave very informative sermons and really wanted to remain at St. Peter's but was soon transferred. He was well liked by most of the congregation who were very disappointed when he left. Parishioners liked his way of teaching as he gave his Sunday sermons. Each new sermon would build on his previous one.

Father Thomas Crum, ordained in 1975, was appointed pastor on August 13, 1999. He came from St. Charles parish, Boardman. He had also been a faculty member of Youngstown Cardinal Mooney High School. He had served as assistant pastor at St. Mary's, Massillon; St. James's, Warren; St. John the Baptist, Campbell; St. Christine's, Youngstown; Our Lady of Mount Carmel, Youngstown; and Immaculate Conception, Ravenna, with a total of nine former assignments before St. Peter's.

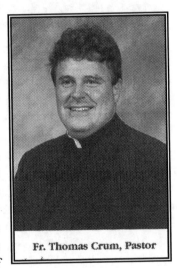

Father Crum loved to garden and cook. During a sabbatical leave, Father attended the Institute of Culinary Arts, Pennsylvania, for two years. He also had some theatrical training and initiated the play *The Passion of Our Lord According to St. John* in 2005. See Chapter XI (Report Section, Report #9) for the Passion play by parishioner Helen White. Father also had a very good tenor voice and loved to sing. During Father Crum's time at St. Peter's, there were several proposed plans put forth concerning the building of

Fr. Thomas Crum, Pastor

more worship space: (1) Relocate the church near Rootstown Center; (2) Relocate 2/10 of a mile southwest of the present church on Sax Road; and (3) Remove the old church and rectory and build a new church and rectory in that approximate location.

Father's method of appointing parishioners to the parish council was a process that certain parishioners did not approve of and did not support. It must be stated, however, that certain other parishioners and non-parishioners did support the process. Several letters were written by parishioners to local newspapers and to the diocese concerning the building issues. These letters were both pro and con and caused much turmoil in the church.

The Rootstown Board of Zoning Appeals had granted a variance concerning the set-back distance from the road right-of-way for the new church building for the present site on Old Forge Road. This variance was also questioned by certain parishioners. On October 19, 2004, legal action was filed in the Court of Common Pleas, Ravenna, Ohio, by a group of parishioners and neighbors contesting the granting of the variance and the use of residential property for commercial purposes of building a church in a residentially-zoned area. During this period of time, there was most definitely a divided parish.

Something very positive did happen, however, during this time. The large cemetery crucifix was painted and repositioned on a new pole and a new roof was constructed. See Chapter XI (Report Section & Photo Section, Report #10 & Photos #29 & #30) for details.

On July 15, 2005, Father Crum was transferred to Our Lady of Peace parish, Canton, Ohio, by Bishop Thomas Tobin, Bishop of Youngstown.

On March 31, 2005, Bishop Tobin was appointed Bishop of the Diocese of Providence, Rhode Island.

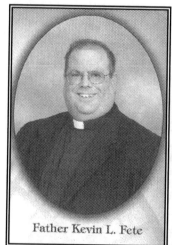

Father Kevin L. Fete

On July 15, 2005, Father Fete came to St. Peter's assigned as Administrator. Father was the resident pastor of the Church of the Little Flower in Middlebranch, Ohio, and also continued in that capacity. Former pastor of St. Peter's, John Sargent, was assisting at Little Flower and the two priests had become close friends.

Father Fete was born October 7, 1957, in Canton, Ohio. He attended St. Joan of Arc Grade School, Edison Junior High School, and graduated from Perry High School, Canton, in 1976. He attended St. Gregory's Seminary in Cincinnati, Moreau Seminary, Notre Dame, and then completed seminary schooling at Mount St. Mary's Seminary, Cincinnati. He was ordained March 30, 1985, by Bishop James Malone. Following ordination, he served as associate pastor at Immaculate Heart of Mary parish, Austintown; St. Joseph's parish, Ashtabula; St. Edward's parish, Youngstown; and St. Paul's Parish, North Canton. Father was also Catechist at Cardinal Mooney High School, Youngstown. He was named pastor of Little Flower Parish, Middlebranch, in 1996. These were all Ohio parishes.

Father Fete was given one year by Bishop Tobin to begin the building of a new church or abandon the project. Father knew of the vast differences of opinions of parishioners, so he set up individual mini-meetings with all groups concerned. With his promise of saving the historic church, the lawsuit was dropped and previous plans for a new church were altered to fit the budget and construction soon began. Total cost upon completion was 2.2 million dollars. See Chapter X for more detailed information on building the new church.

In the fall of 2005, Father Fete authorized the establishment of a Heritage Preservation Committee to preserve the historic church and the parish history. See Chapter XI (Report Section, Report #11) for details of that committee and Chapter XI (Photo Section, Photo #31) for Preservation Committee photo.

The parish was saddened by the death of Father Fete on July 23, 2006. Father died of kidney cancer six weeks after being diagnosed.

Four months later, on November 26, 2006, the new church was dedicated by Monsignor Robert Siffrin. Several priests from the diocese and many who had formally served at St. Peter's came to take part in the dedication Mass. The altar was anointed with holy oil as were the walls of the church with assistance from certain of the visiting priests. See Chapter XI (Photo Section, Photo #32) for Mass celebration.

Father John Michael Lavelle, Pastor of Immaculate Conception Church, Ravenna, Ohio, a close friend of Father Fete's and a former deacon at Father Fete's Church of the Little Flower gave the homily. Father Frank Lehnerd, Pastor Emeritus from St. Edward's, Youngstown, gave a eulogy for Father Fete.

A banquet celebration was then held at the German Family Society, Brimfield, Ohio.

According to Deacon Thomas Shay, Father Fete planned his own funeral right down to the number of candles to be used. He also wanted Matthew Chapter 23 to be read in its entirety. This reading was done by Deacon Shay who said it was Father Fete's message to all who attended his funeral mass. A summary of that Gospel is *Don't just say the Word, but be doers of the Word*. The actual reading took about twenty minutes.

Father Lavelle was appointed by the diocese to oversee the completion of the new church after Father Fete's passing.

Father Robert Miller | Father Wilhelm Malasi | Father Peter Siamoo

Three other priests had assisted Father Fete at his Little Flower Church and later assisted at St. Peter's after Father's passing. They were Father Robert "Bob" Miller, Father Wilhelm Malasi, and Father Peter Siamoo. These last two priests were from Africa, visiting the United States as they completed their studies at nearby universities. They assisted with the Masses at St. Peter's until September 2006 when Father David Misbrener came. Frs. Miller, Malasi, and Siamoo gave many thought-provoking and informative sermons. Father Peter Siamoo was comical at times, and one snowy winter Sunday when he was late arriving for Mass he said, "You have five seasons around here—summer, fall, winter, spring, and SNOW." Father Miller, as he would begin his sermons, would always throw out his arms and say very loudly, "Good Morning!" Father Malasi was quite an intellectual priest and one could learn quite a lot about the Catholic faith from him.

On September 15, 2006, prior to the new church dedication, Father David Misbrener was appointed Administrator at Saint Peter's.

Father Misbrener graduated from Greensburg, Ohio, Elementary School and, in 1984, from Archbishop Hoban High School. He studied at Borromeo Seminary, Wickliffe, Ohio, and The Franciscan Monastery, Kennebunkport, Maine. He earned a

B.A. in religious studies at La Roche College, Pennsylvania, in 1991. He also attended SS. Cyril and Methodius Seminary in Pittsburgh. Father was ordained May 7, 1995. He was Assistant Pastor at St. John the Baptist, Uniontown, Pennsylvania, and SS. Peter and Paul, Warren, Ohio. He was also named Administrator of St. Andrew's, Gibsonia, Pennsylvania. In 1998, he was Associate Pastor at Ravenna Immaculate Conception and then in 2002 became Associate Pastor at St. Nicholas, Struthers. On May 3, 2003, he was named Pastor of Our Lady of Victory, Andover, and St. Patrick's, Kingman. Father David Misbrener loves history and music. He plays the organ and accordion and loves to travel to historic sites. Father has had Polka Masses at St. Peter's. Twice since his assignment, he has had adoration of the most Blessed Sacrament with 25 or more area priests and certain out-of-state priests attending.

As stated in Chapter II, on January 30, 2007, Pope Benedict XVI appointed Bishop Murry to head the Catholic Church Diocese of Youngstown. Bishop Murry installed Father Misbrener as pastor at St. Peter's and Jim Massacci as new deacon on August 25, 2007.

Deacon James L. Massacci was born August 26, 1948. He is the son of Louis and Louise Massacci. Deacon James attended school at St. Mary's in Warren, Ohio, until the tenth grade and was then transferred to John F. Kennedy High School, Youngstown, which was newly built. The Deacon had twelve years of Catholic education. He also attended Kent State and Youngstown State Universities. He entered the service on August 22, 1969, and, in 1979, obtained a commission through the Officer Candidate Program. He retired in 1999 while serving as the Provost Marshal for the 99th RSC in Oakdale, PA, which is an Army Reserve component. He married his wife Kathy in 1983. They had two children together; the Deacon has three children from a previous marriage. The children's names are as follows: James Jr., Jessica, Jacqueline, Jacob, and Brenda. The couple currently has four grandchildren; they are Mia, Joslyn, James, David and Ava. Deacon Jim was ordained to the Deaconate in September 2008, after four years of extensive and intensive religious training provided by the Diocese of Youngstown. He is currently serving as a Deacon at St. Peter of the Fields. He also served as professor of Military Science in the ROTC program at Akron University.

Religious Vocations Other Than Priesthood and Deacons

The first person from St. Peter's to become a Catholic nun was Mary Dorothy Luli. She was the daughter of Mr. and Mrs. George Luli, long-time parishioners of St. Peter's, Rootstown.

Sister Mary Dorothy entered the Sisters of Notre Dame Provincial on February 2, 1958, and took her vows August 16, 1960. Sister entered St. John's College in 1960 and then attended Mary Mount School of Nursing in 1965, graduating in 1969. Sister also taught at St. Peter's in the CCD program. Sister Mary then was assigned to the health care center of the Sisters of Notre Dame in Chardon, Ohio, in 1990 as a staff nurse.

From 1999 to 2009 Sister Mary served as administrator for the Sisters of Notre Dame Health Care Center, Chardon, Ohio. After retiring and since August 2010, Sister has been working at Mary Mount Village, Garfield Heights, Ohio.

The only other person who became a nun was Crescentia Paulus. Sister Paulus was a sister to Ernest and Gertrude Paulus, long-time parishioners of St. Peter's, Rootstown. It was reported that Sister Crescentia most probably attended both St. Joseph's, Randolph, and St. Peter's, Rootstown, during her youth. In 1909, at age seventeen, she entered the Order of Humility of Mary, Villa Marie, Pennsylvania. She became a nun in 1913. Sister died in 1938.

Chapter IV
Societies, Sodalities,
Councils, Leagues, and Special Groups

The list of parish societies, sodalities, councils, leagues, and other special groups speak well for the parish over the 140 years of its existence.

The Altar Society was a group of men who took care of the altar in the very early years of St. Peter's. The Altar Rosary Society, which now takes care of the altar, and The Infant of Prague League were started in 1900 by Father John Boyle, St. Peter's first resident pastor.

Early 1930's and 1940's Altar Rosary Society Members

See Chapter XI (Photo Section) for photos and names of the members of the Altar Rosary Society in the 1930s and 1940s (photo #33).

See also 1968 (photo #34), 1991 (photo #35), 2000 (photo #36), and 2006 (photo #37) and 2010 (photo #38) of later Altar Rosary Society members.

Altar Rosary Society Officers and Members for 2009-2010

Officers:
President/ Funeral dinners- Teresa Arbogast
Vice President/ Funeral dinners- Alice Biltz
Secretary- Caroline Ambrose
Treasurer/ Bazaar- Judi Krieger
Rosary Leader- Kathy Ehasz
Christmas Party- Susan Munger
Altar flowers- Marge Conroy
Sacristan- Ruth Weigand

Members:
Barb Kline
Betty King
Shirley Riemenschneider
Isabel Moore
Claudette Sanders
Slyvia Boden
Mary Cochran
Rose Kline

An Assumption Guild and an Annunciation Guild, off shoots of the Altar Rosary Society met in various parishioners' homes through the years. These were women of the parish and under the direction of Father Delmege who charged them with the recitation of the Rosary.

Milta Biltz, aunt to Isabel Biltz Moore, was Altar Rosary President for many years in the 1930s and early 1940s. The earlier presidents from 1900 to 1930 are not known.

The Holy Name Society was started in 1933 by Father Siegfried W. Heyl. It became very active in the 1940s under Pastor Robert Delmege. The society had fifty-three members at that time. The following is the roster of Holy Name Society members in 1946. (Note: Dues were $1.00 per year.)

Angebrandt, John, Jr.	Kline, Raymond	Moledor, Paul
Angebrandt, John, Sr.	Kline, Roy	Moledor, Porry
Bello, Joseph	Kline, Sylvan	Moledor, Robert
Bildershein, Charles	Knapp, Harold	Moskal, Adam
Bildershein, George	Knapp, Oliver	Moskal, Paul
Bildershein, Michael, Jr.	Knapp, Oscar	Paulus, Ernest
Biltz, Louis	Knapp, Paul	Polack, Andrew, Jr.
Biltz, Rudolph	Knoch, Francis	Polack, Joseph
Bolanz, Fred	Kropac, John	Reidinger, Paul
Eichler, Clem	Kropac, Paul	Rodenbucher, John
Englehart, William	Leyland, Harry	Schrader, William
Esposito, Gartano	Luli, George	Smith, Charles, Jr.
Esposito, Louis	Luli, Joseph	Smith, Glen
Hieber, John	Luli, Robert	Smith, Kenneth
Kline, Cletus	Luli, William	Smith, Philmore
Kline, George	Lynch, Daniel	Stanton, Frank
Kline, Gus	Magos, Toby, Jr.	Strickling, Rupert
Kline, Harold	Magos, Toby, Sr.	Winkler, John

<u>Officers</u>: President, Mr. Fred Bolanz; Vice-President, Mr. Cletus Kline; Secretary, Mr. Rudolph Biltz; Treasurer, Mr. Louis Biltz.

See Chapter XI (Photo Section, Photos #39 & #40) for photos of the Holy Name Society.

The Good Seed, a religious weekly for the parish families, dated October 8, 1944, lists the Assumption Guild of the Altar Rosary Society as meeting at the home of Mrs. Perry Moledor. Regular members present were Mesdames Rudolph Biltz, Henry Dussel, Clem Eichler, Sylvan Kline, George Kline, Oscar Knapp, George Luli, John Rodenbucher, Perry Moledor and Miss Gertrude Paulus. Mrs. Emmet Horning and Mrs. Carl Moledor were guests of the Guild. The meeting opened with the recitation of the Rosary. Mrs. Rudolph Biltz was re-elected as secretary. This author was eight years old at this time and personally knew most of the above parishioners. During Father Fowler's time, there were several guilds—all branches of the Holy Family Guild. There was the Rita Ann Guild, a women's social that met at different parishioners' homes; the St. Mary's Guild; the Court of Mary, which was established for young women graduated from high school, but not yet married; the Children's Sodality for young boys and girls; the Royal Club for girls only; and the Rockne Club for boys only. The following is from the July 23, 1967, *Gleanings*: "St. Rita Ann Guild will meet at the home of Mrs. Charles Smith, Wednesday, July

26, 8:00 PM. Please bring scissors, needle and thread for cancer bandages." See Chapter XI (Report Section, Report #12) for an interview of long time parishioner Audrey Kissel Smith.

In an interview with Isabelle Biltz Moore, it was learned that the Girls Club went to the New York World's Fair and Washington D.C. These trips were paid for partially by the parents but mostly by Father Fowler's parents. The Boys Club met weekly and had baseball games. Some were played at Rootstown School.

The adult groups shared cooking recipes, made Christmas cribs for children, and conducted other social type events.

The League of the Sacred Heart, the Catholic Youth Organization (CYO), the Parish Co-op and the Knights of Columbus Council 5173 were instituted by Father Joseph Tomasch in the 1950s.

In the 1960s, under the pastorate of Father Patrick Gallagher, the St. Ann, St. Catherine, St. Martha, St. Odila, St. Rita, St. Mary, and St. Theresa Guilds were formed. A Christian Mothers' Society was added in 1967. See Chapter XI (Report Section, Report #13) for a list of members. This report is in its original format.

The Altar Rosary Society, the CYO, the Infant of Prague, RCIA, and Knights of Columbus are still very active. A Social Justice Committee was established in January of 2005 by Sister Regina. The committee assists local groups in support of those in need. It also selects speakers on religious topics open to all members of the community. The first speakers' program was by Deacon Jim Massaci on prison ministry presented on January 8, 2009. Other programs presented included topics on Family and Community Services by Mark Frisone and Habitat for Humanity by Mary Schaffer. A Safer Futures spokes- person presented information on Domestic Violence, and Christine Craycroft, the Executive Director of the Portage County Park District, also spoke. Euchre card games are also held on a regular basis.

An explanation of the RCIA program or ministry is as follows: RCIA stands for "Rite of Christian Initiation for Adults." It is more of a ministry than a program for people wishing full communion in the Catholic Church. Prior to the 1980s, when an adult wished to receive any or all of the sacraments of initiation (Baptism, Communion, and Confirmation), he or she met privately with the priest for instruction in Catholicism. During Vatican II, the church hierarchy resurrected early church rites that included the faith community. In the early church, those adults wishing the Sacrament of Baptism and/or full communion in the church (the Sacraments of Communion and Confirmation) were brought before the faith community to state publicly their intentions; the faith community was expected to demonstrate through their own lives how to be Christian. Non-baptized adults are called Catechumens, and the baptized (both Catholic and non-Catholic) are called Candidates.

There are "Three Major Rites" celebrated by the candidates and catechumens before receiving the sacraments at the Easter Vigil. They are (1) The Rite of Election; (2) The Rite of Sending Catechumens for Election and Candidates for Recognition by the Bishop; and (3) The Rite of Election of Catechumens and the Call to Continued Conversion of Candidates.

The Rite of Election occurs at the beginning of the catechumens'/candidates' faith journey. They are brought before the community to publicly state their desire to enter into full communion with the church and to study the scriptures.

The Rite of Sending Catechumens for Election and Candidates for Recognition by the Bishop and the Rite of Election of Catechumens and the Call to Continued Conversion of

Candidates are performed on the first Sunday in Lent. The Rite of Sending occurs at the local parish (St. Peter's) with the catechumens signing their names to the sheet marked "The Elect" and the candidates signing their names to "The Candidates" sheet. These papers are taken when the RCIA team and candidates, catechumens and their sponsors go to the diocesan cathedral (St. Columba Cathedral in Youngstown) to participate in the Rite of Election of Catechumens and the Call to continued Conversion of Candidates. The papers marked "The Elect" and "The Candidates" are presented to the bishop, and the catechumens, now called the "Elect," along with the candidates are acknowledged by the bishop and the greater faith community. They will be prayed for publicly by both the local church and the greater diocesan church.

The faithful who celebrate the Easter Vigil and watch the elect/candidates receive the sacraments of initiation have their faith invigorated. Many who have participated in RCIA have gone on to active ministries within St. Peter's. Father John Sargent started the first RCIA at St. Peter's in the early 1980s with Shirley Riemenschneider, Connie Moulton, and Kathy Ehaz assisting him.

The history of the Infant of Prague was explained in depth in Chapter III under Father Boyle's time. There has been an active devotion to the Child Jesus in the parish since that time by individuals and groups. There is presently devotion to the Infant of Prague immediately after morning Mass on certain days.

Several years ago, the Parish youth reenacted The Stations of the Cross titled "It Is Finished" during the Easter season. That presentation is found in Chapter XI (Report Section, Report #14). There is also a devotion to St. John Nepomucene Neumann after weekly Mass on Fridays. The significance of Neumann's role at St. Joseph's, Randolph, in 1841 is covered in Chapter II. Further information on the life of St. John Neumann can be found in Chapter XI (Report Section, Report #6).

Altar or Mass Servers

Serving as an altar boy in the early days of the church was an undertaking of a serious and challenging nature. The priests were stricter, and each altar server had to learn Latin for his responses to the Mass prayers. It was said by many early servers that they could pronounce the Latin words by rote learning, but didn't really know their meaning. Serving Mass in 2010 is quite different because Latin responses do not have to be memorized in most Catholic Churches in the U.S., although there are some exceptions. Perhaps most importantly, females are now permitted to be Mass servers.

It was impossible to indicate the exact years that specific boys served Mass in the early history of the church because church records could not be found. By interview of several now older parishioners, however, approximate years can be established.

Mass servers in the 1920s included John L. Winkler, Paul Reidinger, Cletus Kline, Gus Kline, Jessie Bowen, Paul Heisler, Clarence Hossler, Martin Knipp, Lawrence Winkler, and Clem Ichler.

In the 1930s, Rupert Strickland, Joe McFarland, George Hossler, Paul Knapp, William Knapp, Harold Kline, Louis Esposito, Ernie Paulus, John Rodenbucher, and Paul Reidinger served Mass.

In the early 1940s to the early 1950s, Richard "Dick" Kline, Richard "Dicky" Biltz, Ray and Joe Rodenbucher, Anthony Calabria, George and Bill Luli, William Kelley, Richard Knapp, Jerry Bolanz, John Kropac, Ron Bradley, Chuck, John and Jack Miley, and Chuck Knock served Mass. Here is a list taken from a church bulletin dated July 24, 1949:

August

7	Biltz	Kropac	Luli	Luli
14	Luli	Luli	Kline	Biltz
21	Kline	Biltz	Slimak	Slimak
28	Slimak	Slimak	Rodenbucher	Rodenbucher

September

4	Rodenbucher	Rodenbucher	Biltz	Kropac
11	Biltz	Kropac	Luli	Luli
18	Luli	Luli	Kline	Biltz
25	Kline	Biltz	Slimak	Slimak

October

2	Slimak	Slimak	Rodenbucher	Rodenbucher
9	Rodenbucher	Rodenbucher	Biltz	Kropac
16	Biltz	Kropac	Luli	Luli
23	Luli	Luli	Kline	Biltz
30	Kline	Biltz	Slimak	Slimak

Other servers from 1950-1959 include Ray and Joe Rodenbucher, Robert Winkler (author), John Luli, Roy Kline, Ray Kline, Rupert Strickling, Charles Miley, Ernie Paulus, Bernard Nowogrocki, Richard Kline, and William Luli.

Servers in the 1960s were Joe Rodenbucher, Raymond Luli, Ronnie Knapp, Larry Kline, Richard Biltz, John Kropac, Richard Knapp, Michael Sanders, John Duffy, James Reynolds, Ronald Bradley, Bernard Trares, Otto Fulst, David Nevitt, Larry Adam, David Greenshield, Chuck and John Miley, John and Ronald Slimak, Walter Smith, Harry and Donald Smith, Dennis and Ron Albright, Bob Cook Jr., Dan and John Paulus, Jack and Jim Duffy, and Bob Lux.

From 1989 to 1993, David Conroy, Eric and Scott Ambacher, Jason Moulton, and Josh Hart were Mass servers. There were others, but they could not be identified.

Starting in 1993, special Mass servers for funerals and other occasions such as special celebrations and daily Mass were Bob Lux, Bob Vonstein, Jim Nestich, Roy Paulus, Vern Clapp, and Bill Conroy. Other special servers—serving in 2010—are Peggy Cunningham, Dave Cunningham, Stan Koval, Jerry Biltz, Joe Postlethwait, Joe Guzi, Jim Nestich, David Moore, and David Graydos. Occasionally Tim and Tom Sullivan serve Mass on weekdays.

Some names are listed twice as special servers and regular servers because they did both. The following were servers prior to the present day servers, but again, some of them overlap and continue to serve to date: Rachel Aleshire, Michael Allman, Mark Clark, Adam Craft, Matthew Craft, Amy Crothers, Molly Gut, Joseph Guzi, Joey Hopp, Holly Kibler, Danielle Kibler, Caleb Lemmo, Lindsay Mudd, Sarah Mudd, Molly Muldowney, Wesley Nader, Audry Schroyer,

Zachary Snodgrass, Josh Tatro, Tony Tatro, Nick Tatro, Chad Tatro, Adam Zelina, Kyle Zelina. David Magazzeni was a substitute.

Those who serve Mass today at St. Peter of the Fields are Michael Allman, Adam Craft, Matthew Craft, Amy Crothers, David Cunningham, Eric Dreger, David Gaydos, Joseph Guzi, Alaina Jackson, Holly Kibler, Danielle Kibler, Stan Kowal, Caleb Lemmo, Megan Lemmo, Josheua M'Grath, Adam Moss, Jacqueline Moss, Ronnie Moss, Wesley Nader, Ben Postlethwait, Joe Postlethwait, Will Postlethwait, M. Rodenbucher, Audry Schroyer, Scott Schroyer, Ian Shepardson, Jacob Snodgrass, Jessica Snodgrass, Zach Snodgrass, Josh Tatro, Tony Tatro, Nick Tatro, Chad Tatro, Adam Zelina and Kyle Zelina. Senior servers include Peggy Cunningham, Dave Cunningham, Stan Kowal, Jerry Biltz, Joe Postlethwait, Bob Lux, Joe Guzi, Jim Nestich, David Moore, and David Gaydos.

It should be understood that these lists of Mass servers change from time to time as some leave and others join the team.

Chapter V
Church Choir

As stated in Chapter III, the church was established in 1868, but remained a mission church until the assignment of the first resident pastor Father John Boyle in January of 1899. In Father Boyle's book of records in 1900, he indicates that the "Children's Choir" will sing at the April Devotions to the Sacred Heart of Jesus and again during the May Devotions to the Blessed Virgin Mary. They also sang at the May 1900 unveiling of the Infant of Prague statue which is still displayed in the historic church.

After corresponding with Catholic University of America, Washington, D.C., and conducting several interviews of parishioners, the author learned that the following persons also served St. Peter's as organists and as singers: Louisa Knapp, great aunt to past parishioner John Kenneth Kline and relative to this author, was the organist during Father Lindesmith's time at St. Peter's. Choir members in 1902 were Maggie Knapp, Adam Knapp, Charlie Kline, Barney Wiedeman, Matilda Wiedeman, George Kline, Anna Kline, Henry Dussel and Clara Rothermel.

Clarence Kline, farmer and father of above John K. Kline, was the organist in the early 1920s. Mary Kline, daughter of Henry C. Kline, whose farm was directly across the road to the South from the church, was also an organist. Cathryn Winkler Miller, daughter of John and Margaret Knapp Winkler, was the organist from 1924 to 1928. Cathryn's younger sister Julia Winkler Fitt was the church organist from 1928 to 1932 when she was only 15 years old to the age of 20. She then married and left the parish. Upon moving back to St. Peter's, she played again at the request of Father Fowler. See Chapter XI (Report Section, Report #16) for an interview of Cathryn & Julia. Both of these sisters learned their music from their mother Margaret Knapp Winkler who had her own organ in the Winkler farm house. This writer personally observed this organ as a young lad.

The church organ was pumped by a wooden handle by previously mentioned parishioner and farmer, Ernest Paulus. Marie Bourquin Horning, wife of Paul Horning, was the organist from 1937 to 1943. Her son Dave of Mogadore, Ohio, said when he was about age three, his mother tied him to the leg of the organ so he wouldn't fall down the steep choir loft stairs as she played the organ. Those stairs are still intact today and remain unchanged from their original construction.

Matilda Weidman Biltz, wife of Louis Biltz of Rootstown and mother to Eloise Biltz Sweet of Rootstown, and Mrs. Ray Kline sang in the choir in the 1930s and 1940s. Louis Biltz, named in Chapter III, was the parishioner who took Father Fowler around the parish area to bring back the fallen away Catholics. Louis operated an auto garage and wrecker service for many years at the center of Rootstown.

Elizabeth "Betty" Biltz King, spouse of Gerald King, was the organist from 1944 to 1953. Betty is a sister to Isabel Biltz Moore, Shirley Biltz Riemenschneider, Winifred Biltz Kaltenbach, Mary Katheryn Biltz Knapp, Alma Biltz Winkler, Charles Biltz, and Richard Biltz. (Note: These above names are mentioned because the "Biils," "Bils," "Biltz"—all these spellings were used at certain times—family was one of the largest families at St. Peter's and one of the oldest in the Church's history. All the above were parishioners at St. Peter of the Fields. Betty Biltz King,

Isabel Biltz Moore, Shirley Biltz Riemenschneider, and Winifred Biltz Kaltenbach remain parishioners today (2010).

Mrs. Ray Kline and Sister M. Francis also assisted in the organization of the choir in the 1940s. John Kenneth Kline was the organist from 1954 to 2005, a period of 51 years. According to Mr. Kline, there were seventeen choir members in 1959. Those members and others who joined the choir later were Rose Kline, wife of John Kenneth Kline; Rupert Strickling; John Rohal; Dorothy Smith, daughter to Audrey Kissel Smith; Mary Kay Kline; Helen Ambrose Gless; Ellen Wolford; Betsy Kline; Judy Hendershot; Stanley and Caroline Ambrose; Mary Sober; Ron Albright; Theresa Kline and Mary Francis Kline, both daughters of John and Rose Kline; Carl Columba; Carl Conley; Christine Kline Luli; Thelma Biltz; John Duffy; Linda Kline Esterday; Joan and Marie Rice, twins; Alice Biltz; Dorothy Galzerano Stoessner; the Winkler sisters—Mary Winkler Gorman, Marge Winkler Conroy, Rose Winkler Darling, Helen Winkler Parry, and Gertrude "Trudy" Winkler Shrigley; and brother James Winkler. These last six were children of long-time dairy farmers and parishioners John L. and Marie E. Weigand Winkler, again one of the largest families at St. Peter's. During the research for this history, it was discovered that there is a grave marker in the cemetery with the name "Winklar." It is unknown who this is.

Mrs. Lilly Mae Whittaker, mother-in-law of long-time parishioner and farmer Gerald Turk, was one of the organists starting in 1964. Judy Demkowicz Hendershot began playing in 1966 when Father Allen Simpson came to St. Peter's. When Father John Sargant came in 1981, Judy began playing again and is the present director of the traditional choir. Judy has been playing and directing for nearly 40 years. Christine Ambrose, daughter of Stanley and Caroline Ambrose, played from 1970 to 1972 as a high school student. Dolores Quinn also played the organ from 1955 to 1998 and then, after a two year absence, played from 2000 to 2006. Cornelius Drugan played from 1998 to 2000.

Former parishioners Tina Miley and Terry Hines, former Sisters for Christian Charity, conducted the contemporary choir from 1987 to 2004. Their leadership occurred during Father John Sargant's, Sister Regina's, and Father Crum's time. Choir members were Theresa Arbogast; Steven and Mandy Kline, children of long time parishioners Barbara and Henry Kline; Don Vair; Lori Kilpatric Knapp; and Gary and Mary Alice Navratil.

Alice Biltz began playing in 1983 as assistant to Judy Hendershot and Kenneth Kline and continues to this day as an organist.

Long-time choir members who sang mainly under the direction of John Kenneth Kline and Judy Hendershot included the following: Ron Albright, Betty King, Stanley and Caroline Ambrose, Jim Winkler, Dolores and Robert Winkler, Lauris MacEwen, Brian Ames, Jessica Latch, Marge and Bill Conroy, Vivian and Jerry Forgus, Christine Luli, Claudette Sanders, Alice Biltz, Dick Feran, Steve Clark, Kath Rowland, Helen Parry, Nick Rothermel, Kathy Shrene, Terry Lasko (flute player), and Lizabeth Ott.

Present Choir and Musicians (2010)

Debbie Tatro was the director of the contemporary choir until 2010. Members are Pete Suzelig, now director (guitar), his brother Ted Suzelig (guitar), Ted's wife Syndie (piano), Jay Nader (piano, organ, and steel drums), Terry Laskos (flute), and singers June McCullough, Theresa Arbogast, Holly Clark, Laura Lansinger, and Wilma Arbogast, Amy Crothers, Deanne

Cunningham and Bonnie Panovich. This choir also performs on occasion at St. Joseph's Church, Randolph, Ohio.

Judy Hendershot is the director of the traditional choir. Members are Alice Biltz (organ and piano); singers include Steve Clark, Bill Conroy, Marge Conroy, Dick Feran, Jerry Forgus, Vivian Forgus, Christine Luli, Kenneth Kline (deceased), Rose Kline, Helen Parry (cantor), Nick Rothermel (cantor), Kathy Rowland (cantor), and Susan Sullivan (cantor) who also sings at weekday Masses and other special occasions. Special guest Amanda Paar has also performed on harp for certain occasions. See Chapter XI (Document Section, Document #7) for old church songs and Chapter XI (Photo Section, Photos #41-#49) for 1968, 1991, 2000, 2006 and present day choir photos.

Chapter VI
Catechism Program

Based on early church records and interviews of early parishioners, it is believed that the priests taught the catechism classes up until the early 1900s. Sunday school records dated 1903 from Father Lindesmith list the following as students: Vernon Heisler, Frank Lansinger, Elizabeth Miller, Grace Paulus, Matilda Reidinger, John Reis, Bertha Kline, Clarence Kline, John McFarland, Josephine Schmitt, Rudolph Biltz, Mary Fisher, Elizabeth Weideman, Vernon Kline, Leroy Kline and Ida Bower. The record states that these names are in order of their class standing.

Records dated 1905 from Father Lindesmith list Joseph McFarland, Milton Kline, Allison Saunders, Alice Goother (daughter of Mike Goother, Civil War Veteran), George Gauer, Ervy Kline, Mary Schmitt, Irene Moon, Nina Kissel (sister to Joseph Kissel), Lawrence Moon, Clara Bower, and Henry Bower. Again, these names are in the order as they ranked in class. Father's name on these records is printed as Rev. E.W.J. Lindesmith, Chaplain U.S. Army Pastor.

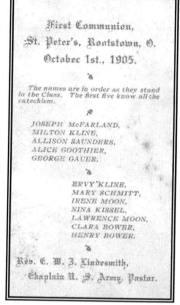

If one compares the names of these children in the Church's catechism program in those early years with the present parishioners, it can readily be seen that the parish has second and third generations of these early members.

With the exception of that already stated from Father Lindesmith's records, there were few early records available regarding catechism classes. The following, however, was obtained from former parishioners. Cathryn Winkler Miller (aunt to this author) said there were ten children in the Catechism program in the early 1920s. Her sister Julia Winkler Fitt (who played organ at age sixteen) said there were ten children in the program in 1926. Alma Biltz Winkler (spouse of Lawrence Winkler, both long-time parishioners) said there were four girls and five boys in the 1930 program.

In the 1940s, the Dominican Sisters from the Immaculate Conception Church in Ravenna, Ohio, came to St. Peter's to give catechetical instruction. An interview with Sisters M. Francis O.P. and M. Concetta O.P. revealed there were 75 children enrolled in 1944 with 21 in high school, 28 in grades 5th-8th, and 28 in 1st-4th. Sisters Agatha Miller and Francis Harding also assisted. In 1945, there were 61 children enrolled, and from 1947-1950, records indicate the program had approximately 62 children each year.

Parishioners scheduled to transport the Dominican Sisters from Ravenna to St. Peter's and back were assigned as follows:

<u>1945</u>
Sept. 23 Bello, Joseph
       30 Biltz, Louis
Oct.   7 Biltz, Rudolph
       14 Bolanz, Fred
       21 Bosko, Peter
       28 Calabria, John
Nov.   4 Dussel, Henry
       11 Eichler, Clem
       18 Esposito, Gaetano
       25 Galzerano, Angelo
Dec.   2 Kline, Cletus
        9 Kline, Gus
       16 Kline, Raymond
       23 Kline, Roy
       30 (no classes)

<u>1946</u>
Jan.   6 Kline, Sylvan
       13 Kline, William
       20 Knapp, Oscar
       27 Knoch, Francis
Feb.   3 Kropac, John
       10 Kropac, Paul
       17 Leyland, Harry
       24 Luli, George
Mar.   3 Luli, Robert
       10 Moledor, Perry
       17 Moskal, Adam
       24 Paulus, Ernest
Apr.   7 Rodenbucher, John
       14 Serva, Stephen
       21 (no classes)
       28 Smith, Glen
May   5 Smith, Philmore
       12 Stanton, Frank
       19 Strickling, Rupert
       26 Winkler, John

Substitutes were listed as:
    George David, Jack Nemet, Robert Moledor, Daniel Lynch, Oliver Knapp, Mrs. Paul Huth, Mrs. George Boucher, Miss Clem Bosko, Miss Mary T. Esposito, and Miss Evelyn Moskal.

    In 1950, Pastor Robert Delmedge made arrangements with Father Frederick Bertran, St. Joseph's, Randolph, and Reverend Emmett Walsh Bishop of the Youngstown Diocese to have the Sisters of Notre Dame from St. Joseph's, Randolph, teach the children. The Church records show 60 children (29 boys and 31 girls) in 1950, 57 children (25 boys and 32 girls) in 1951, 63 children (28 boys and 35 girls) in 1952, 61 children (30 boys and 31 girls) in 1953, 64 children (33 boys and 31 girls) in 1954.
    The weekly church paper, *The Gleaning,* dated September 23, 1951, reported 65 children in Sunday school as follows:

<u>Lower Grades: Sr. Mary Floracine, SND</u>
<u>1st Grade:</u>
John Rice, Dorothy Smith, Gertrude Winkler
<u>2nd Grade:</u>
Ronald Bradley, Christine Kline, David Moore, Sharon Wolford

3rd Grade:

3<u>rd</u> Grade:

Larry Kline, Ronald Knapp, Charles Miley, Helen Winkler
4<u>th</u> Grade:
Raymond Luli, Joan Rice, Marie Rice, Rosalind Winkler, Gerry Wolford

Middle Grades: Father Delmege
5<u>th</u> Grade:
John Esposito, Linda Kline, William Moskal, John Serva, Pamela Strickling, Mary Wolford
6<u>th</u> Grade:
Carol Kline, Dorothy Luli, Virginia Rickard, Marjorie Winkler
7<u>th</u> Grade:
Henry Kline, Rosemary Knapp, Ralph Polumbo, Edward Rodenbucher, James Winkler
8<u>th</u> Grade:
Phyllis Bradley, David Knapp, Charlene Kropac, Peter Polumbo, Dolores Rickard

Upper Grades: Sr. Mary Apolline, SND
9<u>th</u> Grade:
Ray L. Knapp, Mary Luli, Ronald Slimak, Mary Winkler
10<u>th</u> Grade:
Christine Angebrandt, Elizabeth Angebrandt, Edward Bildershein, Elizabeth Esposito, Dorothy Galzerano, Thelma Kline, Martha Knoch, John Luli, John Slimak, Nancy Verk, Robert Winkler
11<u>th</u> Grade:
Ray W. Kline, Elizabeth Knapp, Shirley Mullins, Madeline Rowe
12<u>th</u> Grade:
Shirley Biltz, Richard Kline

Lower Grades: 16
Middle: 20
Upper: 21
Total: 57
Not in Sun. School: 8
Total: 65

From 1955 to 1963, there was an average of 23 boys and 19 girls in the CCD program. During Father Simpson's time, from 1964 to 1968, there was an average of 17 boys and 18 girls in CCD. Below is a list of parishioners scheduled to transport Sisters from St. Joseph's as listed in the church bulletin of Sept. 1965. Note the new parish family names that appear contrasted with earlier records.

Mrs. Edward Clinic
Daniel Albright
Van Note Black
Raymond Bradley
Samuel Catalona

William Conley
Cornell Curtician
August Embacher
Mrs. David Goodhart
Donald Hillegas

Paul Hucovsky
Gerald King
Ray W. Kline
Russel J. Kline
Mrs. Ann Kuzma

Mrs. Kenneth McCullough
Charles E. Miley
John P. Miley
Robert Mullaly
William Pletzer
Edward Pollack
Francis Reese
Joseph M. Schaefer
George J. Schuster
Arthur Schwartz
Stephen A. Serva Jr.
Ronald Sharpless

Paul Teats
Gerald Turck
Robert Turso
Jack Wymer
William Zdanczewski

Substitutes:
Donald Armbruster
William J. Kline
Ray W. Kline
John Luli
Elmer Riemenschneider
Lawrence Postlethwaite
David Woolf
Lester Wise
Walter Knapp
James Winkler
Henry Kline

Father Michael Gawron served from 1968 to 1981. During this period of time, late 1960s to late 1970s, CCD teachers were Rose and Kenny Kline, Audrey Kissel Smith, Shirley Biltz Riemenschneider, Judy Demkowicz Hendershot, Patricia Knapp, Ronald Brooks, Carl Conley, Steve Amato, Robert Strickling, Roy Paulus, John Rohal, Phyllis Bradley Loudin, Marge Winkler Conroy. The principal was Helen Gless who served from 1960 to 1978. See Mrs. Gless's letter to her staff in Chapter XI (Letter Section, Letter #4). Joe Grahm served as principal from 1977 to 1981.

Father Sargent served from 1981 to 1995. During this period, CCD teachers were Cathy Embacher, Kathy Ehaz, Shirley Riemenschneider, Pat Sever, Dave and Connie Moulton, Sue Jenior, Marge Conroy, Harriet Rorar, Caroline Ambrose, Sharon Flint, Jim Ward, Debbie Jakubisin, Debbie Hyatt, Sherry Shay, Debbie Scott, Karen Ridenor, Ester Koval, Steve Quinn, Cheryl Lawson, Cathy and Dennis Hopp, Lyn Hendershot, Nancy Dutko, Paul Kreiger, Judy Kreiger, Deena Engle and Charity Lemmo.

Specific church records could not be located for the years 1981-1984. The following information, however, is specific for the years 1985-1989. Mr. Robert Walker was principal for the years 1985 to 1987, and Paul Krieger served as assistant principal. Staff and teachers for the 1985-86 school year were:

Connie Moulton- Individual Life Chairperson
Rose Ann Newell- Secretary
Judy Kreiger- Office Aide
Elizabeth Sanders- Custodian
Melanie Riemenschneider- Pre-School
Linda Sanders- Kindergarten
Mary Benich- Grade 1
Shirley Riemenschneider- Grade 2
Kathleen Brodie- Grade 3
Alice Biltz- Grade 4
Kathy Ehasz- Grade 5
Bernice Clapp- Grade 6

Kathie Embacher- Grade 7
Harriett Rorar- Grade 8
Connie Moulton- Grade 9
Raymond Knispel- Grade 10
Mary Caspary- Grade 11
Steve Amato- Grade 12

Substitutes were listed as:
Patricia Albanese- Intermediate
Kathy Benich- Elementary
Deena Engle- Primary
Jim Menegay- All Grades
Rebecca Wawrin- Pre-School; Grade 6
Mr. Russel Newell served as principal for the 1987-1988 school year.

The CCD staff for 1988-1989 was as follows:
Shirley Riemenschneider- Christian Formation
Ted Embacher- Principal 1-8
Paul Krieger- Assistant Principal 1-8
Rose Ann Newell- Secretary
Barbie Benich- Pre-School
Janet Berta- Kindergarten
Michaelann Meloy- Grade 1
Jennifer Pospichel- Grade 2
Becky Bailey- Grade 3
Ester Koval- Grade 4
Kathy Ehasz- Grade 5
Bernice Clapp- Grade 6
Kathy Embacher- Grade 7
Kathy Drugan- Grade 8
Connie Moulton- Co-Principal 9-12, Grade 9
Tina Miley- Co-Principal 9-12, Grade 10
Steve Francis Jr.- Grades 11 & 12

Substitutes were listed as:
Patricia Albanese
Steve Amato
Deena Engle
Scott Harmon
Dave Moulton

Harriet Rorar
Donna Ward
Jim Ward
Rebecca Wawrin

For the years 1989 to 2010, the CCD staff was as follows:

1989-2001	Ted Ambacher (Elementary Principal)
	Paul Krieger (Assistant Elementary Principal)
	Judy Krieger (CCD High School Director)

1991   Tracy McClure- Pre-school
                      Debbie Jakubisin- Kindergarten
                      Lynn Dillon- Grade 1
                      Sue Jenior- Grade 2
                      Leslie Householder- Grade 3
                      Esther Koval- Grade 4
                      Jack DiFeo- Grade 5
                      Jennifer Flecksteiner- Grade 6
                      Darleen Fetterhoff- Grade 7
                      Kathy Drugan- Grade 8
                      Connie Moulton- Grade 9

2000   Jim Ward (Assistant High School Principal)

2001-2003   Jim Ward (Principal)
                      Debbie Scott (Assistant Principal)

2004-2006   Debbie Hyatt (Religious Education Director)

2006-2010   Marjorie Conroy (Principal)
                      Assistant Principals: Mary Anne and David Brunelle

Parishioners of St. Peter's who are presently teaching the CCD children (2010):

Catechists

Deanne Cunningham
Paula Justice
Harry and Eileen Hagenbaugh
Becky Falatok
Suzanne Gabric
Ron Cantu
Jerry Biltz
Cheryl Lawson (teacher,
  but recently deceased)
Chris Barkhurst

David and Lee Gaydos
Charity Hawkins
Patricia Jones
Theresa Dreger
Nate Dreger
John and Marie Jansen
Teresa Steiniechner
Jackie Devies
Claudette Sanders

Children's Literature
Theresa Dreger
Lynn Moss
Marge Conroy

Staff
David and Marianne Brunelle
Marge Conroy
Dave Cunningham

Substitutes
Judy Hendershot
Ruth Weigand
Shirley Riemenschneider
Sue Buskey
Angela Bechter
Marguerite Amonett

CCD Teachers, 2010
Back row (left to right) Marge Conroy, Nate Dreger, John Jansen, Paula Justice, Teresa Steiniechner, Jerry Biltz, Eileen Hagenbaugh, Ron Cantu, Harry Hagenbaugh. Front row (left to right) Marie Jansen, Suzanne Gabric, Jackie Devies, Claudette Sanders, Marguerite Amonett, Marianne Brunelle, Dave Brunelle.

Present CCD Students (2010)

Preschool:
Lauren Krieger
Sydney Munger
Re'ana Nestich
Dillon Jackson
Preston Bello
Audrey Francis
Matthew Heigelmann
Zackary Dougherty

Kindergarten:
Daniel Camp
Devin Devies
Nickolas Roberts
Will Yount
Daniel Zalamen
Cory Cunningham
Emma Borberly
Brandan Nicholas
Sarah Conroy

First:
Natalie Coduta
Ally Glass

Joey Yount
Jeffery Pihlblad
Landon Amonett
Faith Cole
Andrew Pringle
Carter Hockin

Second:
Lydia Bartek
Savannah Munger
Alyssa Reinagle
Mariah Cunningham
James Cole Nestich
Jaiden Harris
Brandon Heigelman
Katliyn Wiegart
Dawson Moore
Quincy Powers
Hannah Dougherty
Coulton Michale

Third:
Kylie Camp
Owen Carlson

Livia Coduto
Garrett Formick
Lauren Glass
Hannah Justice
Molly Postlethwait
Nicholas Putnam
Dominique Rimar
Cecila Savage
Tony Connelly
Bryan Zalamea
Garrett Johnson
Isaiah Schweizer
Anna Ford

Fourth:
Justin Devies
Isaac Foster
Troy Cable
Jessica Craft
Adam Helmling
Savanna Dreger
Aaron Weingart
Ciara Cooper
Shayla Clegg
Jenny Consolo
Grace Gretz
Marci Postlethwait
Toriana Harris
Kaleb Dulaney
Ian Joseph Bartek
Kyle Borbely

Fifth:
Daniel Coduto
Dominic De Salvo
Megan Donnelly
Carol Foster
Madeline Heater
Kyle Pruitt
Chandler England
Jenna Sturm-Moulton
Nicole Nowak
Nick Connelly
Bryce Donelus

Mackenzie Moore
Seth Johnson
Ryan Wilson

Sixth:
Morgan Allman
Brandon Baldwin
Madaline Buskey
Joseph Camp
Danielle Carlson
Caitlyn Franczkowski
Matthew Goodyear
David Rimar
Jessica Snodgrass
Joseph Weingard
Devin Harris
Carli Autry

Seventh:
Michael Donnelly
Anne Dreger
Tyler Feciuch
Connor Formick
Gabriel Gretz
Amber Helmling
Alaina Jackson
Jacqueline Moss
Will Postlethwait
Chad Rodenbucker
Kimberly Adams
Ashley Cole
Colin Michalec
Ryan Johnson
Jackie Johnson

Eighth:
Nathan Buskey
Anthony Miley
Lewis Muldowney
Zachary Pruitt
Jacob Snodgrass
Anthony Nowak
Austin Wischt
Jillian Fesemyer

AJ Stronz
Makayla Dulaney
Auston Michalec
Steven Pavliga
Adam Craft

Ninth:
Dylan Baldwin
Adam Craft
Donnie Cunningham
Anthony Goodyear
Ronnie Moss
Ian Deffenbough
Cody Autry
Collin England
Brandi Barkhurst
Kaylee Consolo
Kalli Dreger
Heather Franczkowski
Savannah Heater
Amanda Huth
Anna Lynch
Amanda Savage
Emily Dye

Tenth:
Todd Esola
Molly Gut
Hannah Helming
Andrea Knapp
David Magazzeni
Adam Moss
Eugene Muldowney
Ben Postlethwait

Zach Snodgrass
Erin Trantham
Danielle Kibler
Bobby Winkler
Megan Lemmo

Eleventh:
Rachael Alleshire
Michael Allman
Matthew Craft
Amy Crothers
Kelly Fesemyer
Samantha Lynch
Molly Muldowney
Makenna Rodenbucher
Chad Tatro
Taylor Gradowsky
Nate Dreger

Twelfth:
Kyle Barkhurst
Emily Buskey
Kyle Dreger
Lauren Feciuch
Joseph Hopp
Holly Kibler
Amy Ladd
Wesley Nader
Olivia Ward
Jordan Luli
Sarah Cunningham
Venessa Consolo
John Winkler
Corey Autry

Note: It should be understood that the students mentioned above have advanced to the next grade level and the seniors have graduated as of June 2010.

Chapter VII
Church and Surrounding Grounds

As you enter the historic St. Peter's of the Fields Church, a life size statue of the Sacred Heart stands to the right in the vestibule. A large picture of St. Peter walking in the fields hangs on the opposite side of the vestibule; this painting was purchased by Father Robert Delmege in 1941. The stained glass windows in the vestibule bare the names of early parishioners such as Mr. and Mrs. Henry Kline, Mr. Albert Mitsch, Mrs. Mary Mitsch, and Mrs. John Paulus, believed to be the mother of Ernie and Gertrude Paulus. Ernie Paulus was a councilman at St. Peters for eighteen years. Mr. Paulus was one of seven children who grew up on the family farm on the road to Johnny Cake Hollow. The larger stained glass windows in the church proper also bear the names of their donors as follows: Frank and Katherine Marquard (Katherine was the mother-in-law of Cathryn Winkler Miller; Cathryn was one of the early church organists in the 1920s and aunt to this author); George Knapp Sr., brother to Margaret Winkler Knapp (Margaret was this author's great-grandmother); Mrs. George Knapp, sister-in-law to Margaret Winkler Knapp; George and Anna Kline, parents of Clarence, Cletus and Cornelius Kline (these three persons were part of Father McGoogan's band referred to in Chapter III; George and Anna were grandparents to recent parishioner John Kenneth Cline, long time church organist).

Along the walls of the church are the Stations of the Cross. These beautiful stations were purchased in the early 1900s. Past parishioner, Lawrence Winkler, born in 1908, said he and other parish youth went around to the area farmers and neighbors and sold seed, using the money they earned to purchase the stations. They have been refurbished at least twice since their purchase.

Near the altar are the hand-painted statues of Saint Anthony of Padua and St. Joseph. St. Joseph holds the keys to the kingdom in his left hand and the Ten Commandments in his right hand. On the side altar is the statue of Joseph and Mary holding the baby Jesus.

As stated in Chapter III, there is more information on the Infant of Prague statue to share: The 18" high Infant of Prague statue was brought to St. Peter's in 1900 under the direction of the Church's first resident pastor, Father John Boyle. It was touched to the original statue in Prague.

The history of the original statue is quite remarkable. It was a wedding gift from a Spanish woman to her daughter, a Spanish princess who later gave it to the Church in Prague, Bohemia (later called Czechoslovakia). The Prague Church was later destroyed by the Turks. A priest found the statue unharmed in the rubble. The many robes worn by the statue have been given by Royalty including some from China (information gathered from St. Peter's weekly, *Gleaning*, June 30, 1945). It should be noted that Catholics do not pray to, or worship, statues, but they honor and pray to the person that the statue depicts.

The baptismal fountain sits at the front of the church off to the left side. It is very old and was originally piped so that water would flow outside onto the ground as there was no plumbing at its inception.

Certain remodeling took place in 1947 and 1948 when new pews were put in the Church, and the communion railing was removed. See

Chapter XI (Photo Section, Photo #23) for a photo of the communion railing in dark mahogany and (Photo #24) communion railing in white from earlier years.

Outside View: Cemetery and Church Grounds

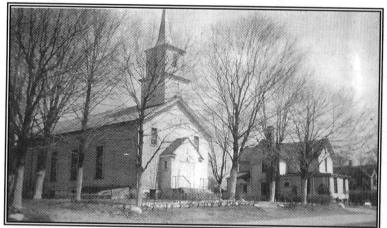

The church building is of post and beam construction built just like the homes and barns of the 1868 era. The bronze cross on the very top of the steeple was mounted so it would turn with the wind much like a weather vane would.

The front entrance was enlarged in 1948 during the pastorate of Father Delmege. On the west side of the Church was a driveway leading back to the cemetery. This driveway was lined with large 2' x 3' x 10" sandstones. The cemetery entrance had a small iron pedestrian gate which swung in both directions. The rows and rows of flowers and bushes were widely known as a show place. As stated earlier in Chapter III, midway into the cemetery on the east side stands the life-size statue of Christ facing west with his arms extended. At the extreme north end of the cemetery is a stone and cement altar and a life-size crucifix of Christ. Review pastorate years of Father Delmedge, Chapter III, for more detailed information on the above two paragraphs.

The handicap ramp on the east side of the church was installed in 1980. Parishioners Charles "Chuck" Biltz, Vernon Clapp, David Jakobison, Elmer Riemenschneider, and certain other men of the parish did the carpentry work.

According to Lawrence Winkler, there was an open shed located on Henry C. Kline's farm directly across the road from the church. This farm was referred to earlier in Chapter III. In the horse and buggy days, parishioners were permitted to park their horses and buggies there during church services. There was a bucket hanging on one of the shed posts for donations. The house and barn still stand, and it is now the Harvey and Marjana Craig Grain and Cattle Farm.

Certain grave markers are of special interest. The tombstone for Michael Bils, 1824-1907, is of the present family of St. Peter's; however, the family name is now spelled Biltz. There was another early spelling of the family name "Biils" as referred to in Chapter III. See Chapter XI for more info on the Biltz family and early Rootstown.

The grave marker for Adam (April 4, 1829- June 6, 1900) and Margaret (September 29, 1838- May 12, 1900) Winkler is also of special interest. Adam was the farmer who sold the acre of land to the church trustees in 1866 for one-hundred dollars. Adam's first wife Catherine died in 1850; his second wife Mary died in 1876. His third wife was Margaret. There is also a very old and broken grave marker with the name Winklar, instead of Winkler. This grave is located on the west side of the cemetery near the front.

The grave marker of Magdalina Rice Kissel, dated March 16, 1867, is also of particular interest. Magdalina was the great-grandmother of parishioner Audrey Kissel Smith. Audrey's grandfather, John Kissel, was a Civil War soldier. For information on other soldiers of the parish, see Chapter VIII.

Another family name, Gouthier, is on one of the church windows. The name is now spelled Goodyear.

Again, these different spellings of the Biltz, Winkler, Rice and Goodyear families should be of great interest to the reader.

Behind the cemetery and to the north was a baseball field constructed by the Knights of Columbus. They also built an open picnic pavilion. This area was much used in the 1950s and 1960s. Today this area is adorned with six foot wooden Stations of the Cross placed there by Robert J. Winkler, son of this author, and Brandon Winkler, grandson of this author.

The original rectory built in 1900 was removed in 2006 to make room for the present new church; however, under Father John Sargent's time, 1981-1995, an attached garage and equipment storage room was added. The basement of the historic church was remodeled into several classrooms. Much of this work was done under the direction of former parishioner Vernon Clapp. Father Sargent also had insulation installed to protect the large stained glass windows of the church. The kitchen and restrooms were also updated in the parish hall.

Incidentally, Father Sargent loved to ride his motorcycle often going to the post office in Rootstown. The motor cycle fell on Father one time and broke his ankle. The accident occurred after his retirement from the priesthood. See the Pastorate of Father John Sargent in Chapter III for more information.

A side entrance with double doors was also added to the church. The right door led to the altar area, and the left door went downstairs into the church basement. Another door to the extreme north end of the church, east side, leads to the boiler room and storage area. The original side entrance to the church basement and the church sacristy was quite different. See Chapter XI (Photo Section, Photos #52- #60) for miscellaneous photos of the historic St. Peter's Church dated 1948.

Persons buried in St. Peter's Cemetery as of November 2010

Date listed with the name is the date of death.
Front Section- Old Part
Listed south to north starting in the southwest corner and going north as far as the statue on the east side of the cemetery.

		Esposito		
Row 1:			Antonio C.	1956
Baclawski			Teresa M.	1938
	Anna	1950		
	Adam	1938	**Shon**	
			Joseph	1946
Esposito			Katherine	1937
	Mike	1977		
	Josephine	1979	**Bolanz**	
			Harold	1934

Ehret

August   1928

Babrauskas

Peter   1930

Row 2:
Knapp

Adam   1926
Margaret   1923

Bower

Barbara   1945

Miller

Martin 1907
Barbara   1926

Rummel

Louisa A.   1904

Baclawski

Stanley   1927

Bower

Abby E.   1898

Pitz

Geo. M.   1891

Bils

Michael   1907
Mary Ann   1896

Knapp

Iona   1901

Lansinger

George A.   1893

Basell

Joseph   1892

Kline

Anna   1902
George   1954

Kline

George   1883

Knapp

Nickolaus   1887
Anna Maria   1891

Harter

Fred.   1887

Antes

Phillip   1891

Gauer

John   1872

Knapp

Frankie   1877

Bello

Sabato   1925
Joseph   1927

Bach

George   1875

Rice

Magdalena   1867

Palm

Mary   1870

Lanzinger

Barbary

Row 3:
Knapp

George A.   1933
Katherine   1962

70

Winkler

          Adam   1900
          Margaret 1917

Reis

          Catherine 1923
          Valentine 1899

Beyer

          Johann   1900
          Elizabeth 1885
          George   1882

Zeller

          Joseph   1884
          Catharina 1902

Marquart

          Valentine 1888
          Elizabeth 1884

Lansinger

          Mary Anna 1896
          Philip   1879

Bills

          Joseph   1879

Winkler

          Anna M. 1877

Miller

          Gertrude 1872

Miller

          John   1874

Reis

          Valentine 1871

Palm

          John Adam 1871
          Mary Eva 1904

Winkler

          Catherine 1871

Henry

          Joseph   1936

Kissel

          Magdelena 1867
          (first person buried
          in cemetery)

Phillip

          Miller
          Elizeboth

Lamert

          Phillip   1891
          Margaret 1909

Row 4:
Knapp

          Joseph   1925
          Pauline 1946

Riedinger

          Wilhelmine 1918

Riedinger

          Matilda 1916

Kline

          Cletus H. 1969
          George   1954
          Harold   1916
          Anna   1955

Knapp

          Nick   1916
          Mary A. 1927

Heisler

          Catherine 1934
          Joseph   1927

Heisler

        Vernon H. 1922
        Margaret 1962

Engelhart

        Carl 1952

Engelhart

        William 1949
        Sarah A. 1917

Gauer

        Louise 1947
        John 1936

Gauer

        Carrie M. 1915

Kline

        Henry C. 1935
        Elizabeth 1942

Kline

        Vernon J. 1922

Wise

        John C. 1927
        Louise M. 1941
        Alfred 1920

Kissel

        Louis 1955

Kissel

        John 1903
        Barbara 1928

Row 5:
Marquart

        John F. 1930
        Valentine 1934

Schrader

        Katie 1938

Schrader

        Katharina 1917
        Barnhart 1911
        William 1949

Dussel

        Peter L. 1915
        Henry 1922
        Bertha 1970

Dussel

        Mary A. 1911

Marquart

        Mary 1945

Marquart

        Frank 1913
        Katherine 1908

Marquart

        Geo. H. 1925

Winkler

        John 1947
        Margaret 1962
        Margaret 1942
        Gertrude 1907

Gauer

        Charles 1934
        Mary 1941

Gauer

        Frank 1916
        Elizebeth 1907

Lansinger

        Catherine 1950

Lansinger

        Adam 1904
        Nancy 1938

Mitsch		
	Albert	1934
	Mary	1944
Rothermel		
	Cora E.	1907
Knapp		
	Lawrence	1917
	Margaret	1925
May		
	Hermann P.	1904

Row 6:

Knoch		
	Lucetta A.	1932
Knoch		
	Francis J.	1940
Knoch		
	Francis A.	1952
Knapp		
	Adam	1942
	Margaret	1947
Knapp		
	George	1916
Knappp		
	Eva	1912
Knapp		
	Louisa	1935
Fleischmann		
	Maria A.	1924
	Adam	1912
	Adam	1966

Burtscher		
	George J.	1916
Burtscher		
	Cecelia	1938
Biltz		
	George W.	1964
	Emilia C.	1950
Biltz		
	Francis	1912
Biltz		
	George	1909
	Elizabeth	1938
	Albert John	1900
	Clara Mary	1912
Schmitt		
		Lucas
Luli		
	Henry R.	1920
	Theresa	1939
	Edmund	1926
Guthier		
	Barbara	1918
	Michael	1936
Knapp		
	Katherine	1917

Row 7:

Hostler		
	Valentine	1964
	John	1932
	Katherine	1939
Kline		
	John B.	1923
	Catherine	1918

Guthier
    John J. 1965

Guthier
    Francis 1921

Hostler
    George 1965
    Louise 1920

Habraken
    Rita 1929

Kline
    Fronie 1921

Bower
    Mary 1927
    Adam 1932
    John 1924

Nemet
    Katherine 1934

Kissel
    Adam 1908
    Cecelia

Miller
    Valentine 1905

Knoch
    Olive J. 1938
    Infant (name unknown)

McKinley
    Alice 1939

Adkinson
    Virginia 1939

Tuma
    Florence 1940

Tuma
    Rowen F. 1943

Whittaker
    Lillie Mae 1987
    Henry J. 1966

Back Section (This section, designated as the new part, starts at the Sacred Heart Statue and goes north)

Row 1:

Bildershein
    Frank 2006

Bildershein
    Ed 1992

Bildershein
    George 2006

Angebrandt
    Infant 1947

Hart
    Josh 1999

Easterday
    John 2010

Monk
    Connie 1902

Miller
    Dorothy 1998

Klaco
    Betty 1901

Konopko
    Matt 1998
    Val 2003

Ladd

        Charles 1997

Camp

        Andrew 2008

Buskey

        Jeff 2009

Collins

        Susanne 2009

Scherer

        Ed 2009

Lawson

        Cheryl 2008

Postlethwait

        Larry 2005

Stall

        Judy 2003

Turk

        Jean 2009

Rodenbucker

        Rita 2003

Row 2:

Brown

        Carl D. 1993

Engle

        Charles 1994

Smith

        Charles 1994

Kline

        Cornelius J. 1977
        Florence M. 1975

Knapp

        Andrew J. 1973

Zeiser

        Frank M. 1972

Kelly

        Robert F. 1970
        Frances E. 1958

Miley

        Catharine Ann 1951

Miley

        Martha J. 1990

Bentz

        Benjamin A. 1974

Bentz

        Elizabeth 1949

McFarland

        Joseph T. 1941

Row 3:

Esposito

        Gaetano 1974
        Rose 1982

Calabria

        John 1975
        Ellena 1984

Greenshield

        Carl D. 1981

Starkey

        Lonnie J. 1983

Ambrose

        Andrew 1994

Kline

        Aloysius E. 1992

Baclawski

        Chester R. 1981
        Joyce 1965

Peterson

        Theodore 1964
        Victoria 1987

Peterson

        Ruth M. 1967

Calabria

        Anthony 1993

Galzerano

        Angelo B. 1968
        Angelina 1984

Nardo

        Vito A. 1964
        Anna M. 1997

Nardo

        Joseph A. 1964

Bello

        Anna 1964

Fulst

        Rudolph O. 1960
        Eura 1978

Row 4:
Moskal

        Paul J. 1957
        Agnes S. 1941

Moskal

        Mary P. 1949

Magos

        Toby Sr. 1973
        Rose 1973

Riedinger

        Paul J. 1983

Gungle

        Adam R. 1986
        Theresa 1986

Biltz

        Charles L. 1986
        Gertrude L. 1994

Robards

        Joseph C. 1973
        Bessie C. 1984

Kropac

        Mabel E. 2000
        John J. 1962

Baumgartner

        Joseph 1969
        Rose A. 1971

Albright

        Adelaide J. 1964
        Norbert J. 1986

Kline

        Gust C. 1964
        Mary Ann 1968

Slimak

        Anne V. 1996
        John C. 1967

Row 5:
Riedinger

        John 1939
        Eva 1960

Knapp			Angebrandt		
	William R.	1940		John	1973
				Gerhardt	1991
Knapp			Angebrandt		
	Oscar J.	1959		Franz	1956
	Ollie M.	1990		Regina	1964
Riedinger			Kropac		
	Henry	1982		Paul J.	1983
	Ruth	1957		Mary M.	2005
Bildershein			Kropac		
	Mike Sr.	1962		John J.	1951
	Julia	1985		Katherine	1963
Riedinger			Moledor		
	Lee A.	1996		Perry	1947
	Betty J.	1985		Veronica	1961
Dunford			Biltz		
	Joseph Lane Jr.	1976		Rudolph M.	1963
				Clara M.	1945
Dunford			Winkler		
	Joseph Lane	1965		John L.	1986
				John L.	1943
Lynch				Marie E.	1993
	Evelyn	1985			
	Daniel J.	1968	Luli		
	Mary Jane	1958		Joe J.	1962
Kline				Dora E.	1942
	William G.	1980			
	Florence C.	1993	Lansinger		
				William	1942
Rodenbucher				Flora L.	1959
	John J.	1986			
	Julianna	1973	Biltz		
				Louis E.	1982
Duffy				Matilda B.	1975
	Michael R.	1956			
			Leyland		
Angebrandt				Joseph H.	1988
	John M.	1973		Greta M.	1942
	Christine K.	1992			

Row 6:

Feola
      Paul A. 1940
      Helen L. 1958

Miller
      Andrew 1942
      Catharine 1947

Ambrose
      Thomas 1942
      Antonia 1967

Strickling
      Rupert E. 1975

Kaltenbach
      Robert F. 1982
      Winifred 2010

Kline
      Roy H. 1982

Adkinson
      Vernon 1978

Luli
      Charles S. 1991
      Mary L. 1984
      George H. 1984

Mihalik
      Mark Allen 1981

Gies
      Renee Marie 1992

Gies
      Patricia A. 1972

Mosher
      Helen F. 1965

Kline
      Sylvan J. 1971
      Beatrice 1988

Caprez
      Christina L. 1972

Biltz
      Richard M. 1964

Darrah
      Chester R. 1988

Geib
      Jeffrey L. 1969

Darrah
      Mildred M. 2006

Geib
      Jeffrey Lynn 1969

Schwartz
      Paul R. 1966

Mickunas
      Susan 1965

Weideman
      Richard J. 1965

Biltz
      Thelma 2007

Sweet
      Eloise 2004

Weigand
      Fred 2001

Row 7:

Caspary

      Raymond V. 1971

Fowler

      Reverend Walter 1941
         (only Priest buried in
         St. Peter's Cemetery)

The following are around the back part of the cemetery directly in front of the crucifix and alter. Most are infants.

Calabria

      Charles Anthony 1960

Knapp

      John T. 1955

Kline

      Mary 1961

Kline

      Dale J. 1954

Slimak

      Michael 1958

Kline

      John Jr. 1959

Kline

      Dale J. 1957

Rice

      Andrew 1982

Caspary

      Raymond 1971

Putnam

      Kaitlyn 2003

Deacon Tom Shay was buried in St. Peter's cemetery December 2010.
Charles Miley was buried in St. Peter's cemetery December 2010.

Chapter VIII

Military Veterans from St. Peter's

No greater tribute can be paid to human beings than that bestowed on those who have served or are presently serving in our armed forces. Because of these veterans, we can live in a free society to worship and live as we choose. This chapter contains the names of all known veterans from St. Peter's who served in the various branches of our military from the Revolutionary War to the present day (2010) War On Terrorism.

The Rootstown Centennial Report, January 25, 1944, lists the following veterans who were from St. Peter's and served in the military through WWI:
(A) = Wounded in Action twice
(B) = Honorably Discharged
(C) = Killed in Action

Adam Winkler	Mexican War of 1846
Adam Lansinger	Co. "G" 115 Civil War
Peter Englehart	Co. "H" 184 Ohio Vol. Inf. Civil War
Peter Dussel	Co. "H" 184 Ohio Vol. Inf. Civil War
Michael Guthier	Unknown Ohio Vol. Inf. Civil War
John Bissel	Unknown Ohio Vol. Inf. Civil War
John Kissel	Unknown Ohio Vol. Inf. Civil War
John Hostler	Unknown Ohio Vol. Inf. Civil War
Michael Eck	Unknown Ohio Vol. Inf. Civil War
Robert Biltz	WWI
Gust Kline	WWI

Father Robert Delmege, not Listed in the Centennial Book, but was a WWI Vet.

According to church records dated 1944, the following served in WWII; except where noted, all were (B) = Honorably Discharged

Stanley Ambrose
Charles Bello
Charles Bildershein
George Bildershein
Michael Bildershein
John Caprez
Albert Esposito
Joseph Esposito

Louis Esposito (A)
Paul Huth
William Kelley
Harold Kline
Harold Knapp
Paul Knapp
Roy Knapp
John Leyland (C)

John Moledor
Paul Moledor
Andrew Polack
Joseph Polack
Benjamin Thompson
Victor Placo

Present church members who have served in the military

Steve Amato	US Navy
Paul Amonett	US Army
Jerry Biltz	US Army
John A. Calvarese	US Air Force
Dayton L. Clark	US Navy
Bill Conroy	US Air Force Res.
David Cunningham	US Air Force
Jerry Forgus	US Coast Guard
Steve Francis	US Army Airborne
Richard J. Gray	US Army
Harry Hagenbaugh	US Navy
Bill Housholder	US Army
Gerald King	US Army
Ray W. Knispel	US Navy Res.
Robert Lamm	US Navy
Walter Laskos	US Merchant Marines
Bob Lux	US Navy-Army
James L. Massacci Sr.	US Army
Kathy M. Massacci	US Army
Charles E. Miley	US Army
David M. Miley	US Army
Chuck Miley	US Air Force
Victor Placo	US Navy
Edward Polack	US Army
Tom Pope	US Air Force
Elmer Riemenschneider	US Army
Richard Rodenbucher	US Navy
Harry E. Rorar	US Army
Edmund Scherer	US Air Corp. -Deceased
Raymond Sever	US Army
Tom Shay	US Army
Rich Sholtis	US Air Force-Air Force Reserve
Donald Paul Smith	US Army
Richard Szware	US Marines
Brian Toohey	US Navy
Barney Trares	US Army
Pat Tummel	US Air Force
Peter Twark, Jr.	US Army
Robert J. Weaver	US Army Airborne
James Weingart	US Coast Guard
John W. Winkler	US Navy Reserve

Robert F. Winkler	US Army Airborne
Robert J. Winkler	US Navy
Jeffrey S. Beard	
Shawn Diefendorff	
Sean Francis	
Brian Hickman	
Mike Kliebert	
Jason Ludovico	
Joanne Szwarc	
James McDougal	
John Pollach	
Jeremy Streem	
Aaron Sanders Warman	
Jacob Massacci	

Present church members now serving in the military

Note: These names are as listed in the church weekly bulletin. Certain members have been honorably discharged. The country listed denotes where they served at some time during their obligation.

Charlie Best
Joe Burke
John Duffy
Jason Haney
Justin Jarvis
Jonathan Kercenneck (Iraq)
Justin Newman
Brandon Winkler (Afghanistan)
Ramona M. Wohlwen
Adam Molai
Rachel Stronz
Shane Bennett

Veterans who are buried in St. Peter's Cemetery

Adam Winkler	1829-1900	Mexican War
Joseph R Sanders	1925-1998	WWII
Michael Guthier	1853-1918	Civil War
Michael Klein	1845-1936	Civil War
Larry M. Miller	1947-1998	Vietnam War
Joseph L. Dunford	1925-1965	WWII
Robert F. Kaltenbaugh	1919-1982	WWII

Vernon P. Adkinson	1920-1978	WWII
Gerhardt Angebrandt	1921-2005	WWII
Joseph Baumgartner	1896-1968	WWI
Roy H. Paulus	1930-1996	Korean War
Jeffrey L. Geib	1947-1969	Vietnam War
Chester R. Darrah	1926-1988	WWII
Richard J. Weideman	1921-1965	WWII
Fredrick B. Weigand	1932-2001	Korean War
Benjamin A. Bentz	1891-1974	WWI
Charles R. Ladd	1932-1997	Korean War
Matt F. Knopka	1920-1998	WWII
Larry R. Postlewait	1935-2005	Cold War
Anthony Calabria	1920-1993	WWII
Frank Zeiser	1928-1998	WWII
John E. Mihalik	1939-2001	Vietnam War
Herman Miller	1923-1998	WWII
Walter A. Laskos	1927-2001	WWII
Aloysius E. Kline	1913-1992	WWII
Carl D. Greenshield	1913-1981	WWII
George Bildershein	1914-2002	WWII
Edward Bildershein	1936-2005	Cold War
Frank Bildershein	1929-2000	Korean War
Carl D. Brown	1927-1993	WWII
John Kissel	1842-1903	Civil War
Adam Lansinger	1842-1904	Civil War
Peter Dussel	1847-1915	Civil War
Adam Winkler	1829-1900	Mexican War
Paul Prichard, Jr.	1927-2007	WWII
Lee Reidinger	Unk.-1996	WWII
John Angebrandt	1931-1991	WWII
John Kropac	1874-1951	WWI
Paul J. Kropac	1907-1983	WWI
Edmund Scherer	1924-2009	WWII
Van Bradley Black	1948-2008	Vietnam War
Thomas Ambrose	1961-2010	Cold War
John Easterday	1932-2010	Korean War

Total Veterans Located: 43

Catholic War Veterans Post 1954

The following is information on a veterans group recently formed at St. Peter of the Fields. This information is printed here because not all the members are parishioners of St. Peter's. This group was formed in April 2009.

The Catholic War Veterans were organized on May 9, 1935, by a former World War I Army Chaplain, Father Edward J. Higgins, of Astoria, New York. They have been recognized and certified by the Department of Veteran Affairs (VA) and authorized to represent the claims of veterans before the appropriate VA rating boards. On August 17, 1984, President Ronald Reagan signed Public Law 98-382 granting a Congressional Charter to the Catholic War Veterans of the U.S.A.—the first and only Catholic organization to be honored with such recognition by the U.S. Congress. The Catholic War Veterans are dedicated to a program of united action to promote the well-being of all veterans, joining hands with other veteran service organizations, whenever and wherever through increased prestige. They influence public opinion, promote good laws, and improve the lot of the veteran. They are pledged to an out-and-out fight against atheistic communism and all other "isms" foreign to our American form of government.

Any person who has served ninety days or more in the military service of the United States and is a good practicing Catholic is eligible to join.

Charter Members are as follows:
1) Stan Ambrose
2) Dave Moulton
3) Peter Twark Jr.
4) Richard Rodenbucher
5) Ray Sever
6) Ray W. Knispel (2009 Commander)
7) James L. Massacci
8) William J. Conroy
9) Robert F. Winkler
10) John Winkler
11) Kathy M. Massacci
12) Tom Shay
13) David Cunningham
14) Joe Weaver
15) George Mendiola
16) Ronald Albright
17) Frank Cisneros
18) Bill Householder
19) Father David Misbrener (Chaplin—not a veteran)
20) Richard Soltis
21) Don Slusser (2010 Commander)
22) Bill Winkler

**Catholic War Veterans participating in a flag-folding ceremony
at a veteran's memorial marker in St. Peter's cemetery.**

How veterans were honored in the Early 20th Century
How veterans were honored in the Early 20th Century
Interview of Irene Lang May on January 31, 1997

In 1924, Irene's father, Clement Lang, was the proprietor of a general merchandise store from 1901 to 1938 in the center of Randolph where the gazebo now stands. He had an open-air, large Buick car and would put as many children as he could in the car and go decorate the graves of veterans. Flags would arrive in a large box from Ravenna. Irene recalled visiting five cemeteries: Christian Church of Randolph; Sand Hill Cemetery; German Reformed Cemetery- by Hillgerts; St. Joseph's and St. Peter's. Her father said once, "Let's go to St. Peter's. I don't think anybody does that."

Note: It was also learned in this interview that a school called Beach Land (1855), was located south of Randolph. That information is covered in Chapter II.

CHAPTER IX
Knights of Columbus

Background Information on the Knights of Columbus

HISTORY
The Knights of Columbus was organized in 1882 by Rev. Michael J. McGivney in New Haven, Connecticut, under the principles of charity, unity, fraternity and patriotism. It was founded upon ideals inspired by teachings of our Catholic faith and has a proud heritage of service to Church, country, and neighbor.

MEMBERSHIP
The Knights of Columbus is the largest organization of Catholic men with 1.5 million members who belong to over 9,700 local councils throughout the United States, Canada, Mexico, the Philippines, Puerto Rico, Guatemala, Panama, Cuba, Guam, the Virgin Islands, the Dominican Republic, and the Bahamas.

CHURCH LOYALTY
For over 100 years, the Knights of Columbus has been distinguished by forthright loyalty to the Holy See and to the hierarchy. Referring to this in a recent private audience, Pope John Paul II personally thanked the Order for "the respect and love which you have manifested toward me as successor of Peter."

FAMILY LIFE
Through programs of family prayer, family participation in the parish liturgy, concern for Christian values in the home, "Family of the Month" and "Family of the Year" programs, days of family recreation and the like, the Knights of Columbus works to defend family life which is under fierce attack from modern secularism.

VOCATIONS
Aware of the dreadful need for priests and religious in today's Church, the Knights of Columbus has a network of state, district, and local council vocations committees actively engaged in fostering Church vocations through prayer and various promotional activities.

CHARITABLE DISBURSEMENTS
Donations to charity—for the needy, victims of disaster, homes for the aged, community projects, educational purposes, gifts of clothing and food—totaled over $94 million last year.

PRO-LIFE
The Knights of Columbus conducts an Order-wide "Crusade for Life" campaign to bring an end to the legalized slaughter of the innocent unborn. Millions of pieces of pro-life literature are printed and made available free of charge to cope with the evils of abortion.

INSURANCE POLICY

The Knights of Columbus has nearly $20 billion worth of insurance in force. A wide variety of low-cost and top-quality programs are available to members and their families—annuities, life, health, accident, hospital and income replacement insurance.

EDUCATIONAL TRUST

A million-dollar educational trust provides a four year college education at a Catholic college for children of members who are killed or permanently and totally disabled (a) from a cause directly connected with a military conflict or (b) as a result of criminal violence in the performance of their duties as full-time enforcement officers or firemen.

STUDENT LOANS

Over 50,000 low-interest student loans, representing over $69 million, have been disbursed to Knights of Columbus members and their families since 1971. Without reference to membership in the Order, student loans are available to priests, brothers, sisters, seminarians and postulants at the college, seminary, and postgraduate levels.

COMMUNITY SERVICE

Last year, Knights of Columbus officers, program directors and committeemen volunteered over 36 million man-hours in community service to youth, hospitals, orphanages, and churches.

CATHOLIC INFORMATION SERVICE

Since 1948 when the program began, the Catholic Information Service has provided free religious pamphlets to millions of inquirers and has enrolled almost 800,000 persons in the Catholic Correspondence Course. In addition, the mailbox is always open to those who need advice and can't bring themselves to ring a rectory doorbell.

ON-THE-SCENE INVOLVEMENT

Among many other projects, the Knights sponsor low-cost housing and activities for the elderly, raise funds for persons with mental retardation and physical handicaps, support parishes, schools and other church-related facilities, and organize scouting.

COLUMBIAN SQUIRES

Order's leadership training program molds young men into influential and articulate Catholic citizens of tomorrow. Over 20,000 Squires belong to 1,000 council-sponsored circles in the United States, Canada, Mexico, the Philippines, Puerto Rico, and Guam.

SCHOLARSHIPS/FELLOWSHIPS

Educational benefits are available to members and their families through the Pro Deo and Pro Patria Scholarships; Canadian, Mexican, and Philippines Scholarship Trusts; and Graduate Fellowships.

St. Peter of the Fields Knights of Columbus, Council #5173

The Reverend Father Joseph Tomasch started the Rootstown Knights of Columbus Council #5173. The Council was chartered on August 6, 1961with long-time parishioner and WWII veteran Stanley Ambrose serving as the 1st Grand Knight. The 29 original members were: S.A. Ambrose, L.A. Aristide, D.G. Armbruster, R.J. Armbruster, W.G. Beard, A.J. Dalziel, D.H. Delin, R.T. Fox Jr., P.R. Gregan, D.R. Kerr, L.R. Kline, R.L. Kline, R.J. Kline, R.W. Knapp, R.P. Knapp, R. Luli, T. Magos Jr., C.E. Miley Sr., P.J. Polumbo, G.L. Rennie, E.W. Rodenbucher, P.S. Teets, J.P. Toffanelli Sr., D.E. Woolf, R.J. Albright, C.A. Bello, R.D. Cook, J.J. Rodenbucher, Rev. John Tomasch, Pastor of St. Peter's. They were installed by District Deputy James Delano. David Woolf, John Rodenbucher and Ronald Albright served as trustees.

Early in its history, the Council built a picnic area immediately to the north of the cemetery at St. Peter's. Electric and water were installed, and a pavilion and tables were constructed. The CYO, Catholic Youth Organization, of the parish assisted in clearing the adjacent area for a ball field. Other activities included presenting anti-drug seminars to youth, chaperoning youth club dances at St. Peter's Hall (which actually benefited the younger generation from all over the county), and assisted in the purchase of radio equipment for the Rootstown Fire Department. The Council assisted Rootstown Middle School students financially with their trip to Washington, D.C. and also gave financial support to the local Boy Scout troop. Assistance was given for the purchase of a movie projector and screen for CCD classes at St. Peter's. Softball equipment was purchased for the CYO. Cheese and butter were distributed to the elderly and needy of the Rootstown area. Assistance was given for many years with the Blood Mobile program at the Rootstown Town Hall. Every year the council has supported and worked the Special Olympics programs for the physically and mentally challenged of the county. The "Punt, Pass and Kick" project for youth has also been supported. Youth campaign ticket sales, parking cars at the Randolph Fair, selling Christmas trees, pancake breakfasts on Memorial Day (veterans free), card parties, and other special events help raise funds to do the work of the Knights.

List of Grand Knights
(Appointments of Grand Knights run July to July except as noted.)

1961-62	Stanley Ambrose	1979-80	Dan Conley
1962-64	Charles Miley	1980-82	Carl Conley
1964-66	Robert Smith	1982-84	Frank Cisneros
1966-68	John Duffy	1984-85	Paul Marva
1968-70	Roy Paulus	1985-86	Dennis Samblant
1970-72	Donald Armbruster	1986-87	John Duffy (District Deputy)
1972-74	Robert Armbruster	1987-88	Carl Conley
1974-76	Ronald Armbruster	1988-90	Gerald Biltz
1977-78	Roy Paulus	1990-91	Don Kerr
1976-78	John Duffy (also District Deputy)	1991-92	Paul Marva
1978-79	Greg Urchek	1992-93	Ron Albright
1979-80	Charles Miley	1993-95	Paul Durbak

1995-96 Edward Rodenbucher	2002-04 Scott Riemenschneider	
1996-97 Jim Albright	2004-08 Doug Palmer	
1997-00 Eugene Muldoney	2008-present David Gaydos	
2000-02 Rudy Tosenberger		

See Chapter XI (Photo Section, Photos #75- #97) for photos of the Grand Knights as listed here. Some photos were unavailable.

List of Present Members as of 2009

Adelman, Joseph J	Feran, Richard T	Marva Sr, Paul A
Adelman, William E	Francis, Keith M	Marva, Steve D
Albright, James M	Francis, Matthew J	May, James C
Albright, Ronald G	Franczowski, Ronald P	McCullough, Douglas W
Ambrose, Stanley A	Gay, Timothy	Mercury, Joseph J
Armbruster, August J	Gaydos, David M	Miley Sr, Charles E
Banjazek, Mark J	Gnandt, Joseph T	Mueller, Arthur J
Biltz, Gerald L	Guappone Sr, Vito M	Muldowney, Eugene L
Biltz, Michael C	Guzi, Joseph T	Muldowney, Eugene L
Biltz, Thomas M	Hart, Ronald O	Muldowney, Michael J
Black, Van Note B	Helming, Jeffrey C	Muldowney, Shawn R
Borbely, Brandon A	Hopp, Denny J	Munger, Brian K
Cisneros, Frank	Housholder, William J	Palmer, Douglas E
Cisneros, Greg	Jenior, Lee L	Riemenschneider, E L
Conley, Carl E	Kassell, John P	Riemenschneider, Scott
Conroy, William J	Kerr, Donald R	Rodenbucher, Edward W
Cook, Robert D	King, Gerald R	Rodenbucher, Keith D
Cubon, John A	Kitakis, Kevin J	Samblanet, Dennis L
Cunningham, David B	Kline, Gerald M	Sever, Raymond D
Cunningham, Kevin L	Kline, John K	Shay, Thomas R
Drugan, Cornelius B	Kline, Russell J	Smith, Robert H
Cunningham, Kevin L	Kline, William	Solema, Timothy J
Drugan, Cornelius B	Knapp, Raymond W	Steiner, William G
Durbak Jr, Paul J	Knapp, Ronald P	Timko, Stephen A
Durbak, Joseph M	Koval, Michael G	Tomko, Gordan L
Dussel, Christopher J	Kowal, Stanley J	Tosenberger, Rudy
Dussel, Mike P	Krieger, Greg	Twark Jr, Peter
Edington, Craig S	Lettieri, Luigi	Winkler, Robert F
Feciuch, Larry E	Lucas, Charles J	
Feciuch, Ronald J	Mahony, Mathew L	

Chapter X
New Church Construction

As stated in Chapter III, Father Kevin Fete was given one year to determine if a new church could be built at St. Peter's. After much interviewing and decision making and providing information to the parishioners was completed, the capital campaign or building fund began to excel. Several pastoral council meetings occurred and decisions were made concerning the building plans.

A parish meeting was held to determine by vote what the interior furnishings would be for the church. Under Father Fete's close and decisive supervision, the new church was built just east of the historic church with groundbreaking occurring January 5, 2006. This was the first new Catholic church to be built in Portage County in a decade. Present at the groundbreaking were certain church leaders and approximately 50 parishioners who stood in a cold rain for the ceremony.

Listed left to right is Don Allmon- Chairman of the Building Committee, John Falatok- Building Committee, Debbie Hyatt and Barb Rigenbacker- Pastoral Council, Robert Siffrin- Monsignor, Rev. Robert Miller- Parish Eucharistic Celebrant, Tom Shay- Parish Deacon, and Rev. Kevin Fete- Parish Administrator. In the background are three unnamed servers.

Judy Hendershot provided organ music in the church prior to the ceremony. At about 4 PM the ceremony was begun in the original 1868 church with the clergy and altar attendants processing from the rear of the church while "Praise God from Whom All Blessings Flow" was sung by all led by Judy Hendershot and Helena Parry. Monsignor Siffrin gave a greeting followed by some prayers. Then everyone processed out the rear of the original church to the outdoors to the ground in front of the hall where the processional hymn "Sing a New Church" was completed. The rain drizzled down upon the crowd as Debbie Hyatt read Corinthians 10: 1-6, followed by a Responsorial Psalm led by Judy Hendershot. Then Father Fete read Matthew 16: 13-18 followed by a homily given by Monsignor Siffrin. After the ground was blessed by Monsignor Siffrin, the "Our Father" was recited by all. Petitions were read by Deacon Tom Shay with "Bless and watch over your church, O Lord" as the response. The groundbreaking ceremony was completed by the Clergy, the Building Committee and the Finance Committee Chairman. The gold colored shovels were brought to the area. Father Fete, Father Miller, Monsignor Siffrin, Debbie Hyatt, Don

Allman, John Falatok, Barb Rickenbacker and Deacon Shay spaded up new ground. Representatives from Architect/Planners, LTD, from Cleveland were also present. The closing song was "Send Forth by God's Blessing." Following the ceremony, everyone was invited into the hall for refreshments prepared by the Church Altar Rosary Society.

The outside and inside of the new church are striking. The church is built of red brick, cement block and steel construction. Each pilaster, which can be seen from the outside, has a cross made from darker colored brick. In the court yard to the east stands a statue of St. Peter. Another statue of St. Peter stands in the space between the new church and the historic church to the west. This statue is very old (1945) and, as previously mentioned in Chapter III, stood on the west side of the historic church, prior to being moved in 2008. This statue was scraped and painted in 1996 by brothers Jim and Bob Winkler.

The interior of the new church carries the theme of St. Peter the Apostle. It has gray floor tile and Italian mosaics for Stations of the Cross, which cost approximately $50,000. On the end of each of the church pews (total cost of $107,000) is a carved upside down cross with the keys of St. Peter superimposed over it. History tells us that St. Peter was crucified upside down at his request. He said he wasn't worthy to be crucified up right as his Lord was. The massive altar is gray marble and weighs eight tons. The baptismal font, the ambo and the holy water basins are also of gray marble. The beautiful gold-plated Tabernacle cost approximately $17,000. The church seating capacity is approximately 450 people. The rear of the church can be made to seat another fifty. The eight-foot round stained glass window in the sanctuary is a replica of the one at the Vatican in St. Peter's Basilica. It has been described as the soaring dove of peace in a sunburst, symbol of the Holy Spirit. Father Fete decided on the window design after a discussion with parishioner Joan Reisig, who told him about this window at St. Peter's Basilica in Rome. J.H. Winterich, Inc. was chosen to make the window. An eight-foot round window cover was installed to protect the stained glass. The cost of the window was approximately $40,000 and is one of the hallmarks of the new church. One can appreciate its beauty when the sun's rays stream through it.

The hall, as stated in Chapter III, built in 1959, was incorporated into the new building with space for new offices and classrooms on its east side. The entire roof line is straight which makes everything look like one new building.

A life-sized Sacred Heart statue stands at the rear of the church with its votive candles. A beautiful statue of the Virgin Mary stands in the left front corner, and the Infant of Prague statue is in the back with its votive candles. A large mosaic picture of the Blessed Mother hangs on the wall to the left of the Tabernacle at the front of the church. A large picture of a radiant Jesus hangs on the wall behind the main altar and under the eight foot stained glass window. This painting is based on the story of St. Faustina and the Divine Mercy Chaplet of Prayers.

St. Faustina Kowalska, a Polish nun, reported that she had a vision of Jesus with rays of mercy streaming from the area of his heart. Jesus told Sister Faustina to have an image painted to represent the vision and to sign it "Jesus, I trust in you." In the year 2000, Pope John Paul II announced at the canonization of this nun that the second Sunday of Easter will be called Divine Mercy Sunday. See Chapter XI (Photo Section, Photos #61-#74) for the new church under construction, Stations of the Cross, Tabernacle, eight foot Holy Spirit window, large crucifix of Christ, radiant Jesus, upside-down crosses at end of pews, the Blessed Mother statue, St. John

Neumann, St. Peter inside the church and St. Peter outside the church, Sacred Heart with outstretched arms, and St. Philomena.

List of contractors who built the church:

Hively Construction Co. Inc. of Canfield, Ohio was the General Contractor.

Earthwork:
L & S Excavating and Trucking, Inc.
Middletown, OH

Hot-Mix Asphalt Paving:
Central-Allied Enterprises, Inc.
Canton, OH

Cement, Concrete, Pavement/Cast-In-Place Concrete:
Mudd Construction
Mogadore, OH

Unit Masonry:
George Wischt & Sons
Kent, OH

Metal Fabrications/ Standard Steel Doors and Frames/ Flush Wood Doors/ Door Hardware/ Signs:
Hively Construction Co. Inc.
Canfield, OH

Rough Carpentry/ Asphalt Shingles/ Siding:
DeCerbo Construction, Inc.
Canfield, OH

Interior Architectural Woodwork:
Crowe's Cabinets, Inc.
Lowellville, OH

Bituminous Dampproofing:
Stacy's Foundation Coating
Columbiana, OH

Building Insulation:
Mooney & Moses
Poland, OH

Joint Sealants:
All Ohio Sealants, Inc.
Canton, OH

Aluminum Framed Entrances/ Glazing:
Liberty Glass & Mirror Co., Inc.
Akron, OH

Wood Windows:
Pella Window & Door Co.
Bedford Heights, OH

Gypsum Board Assemblies/ Acoustical Panel Ceiling:
United Interiors, Inc.
Youngstown, OH

Ceramic Tile:
South Range Tile and Marble, Inc.
Salem, OH

Painting:
Bochert Brothers Painting and Decorating
Poland, OH

Toilet Compartments/ Fire Protection Specialties/ Toilet and Bath Accessories:
W.B. Becherer, Inc.
Boardman, OH

Fire Suppression Piping/ Plumbing Fixtures:
Star Plumbing
Ravenna, OH

Architect Drawing—Steeple:
Campbellsville Industries, Inc.
Campbellsville, KY

Architect Drawing—Dumpster Enclosure:
Anchor Construction Fencing Co., LLC
Eastlake, OH

Architect Drawing—Gutter and Downspout:
Ruse's Seamless Gutters
North Jackson, OH

Mechanical:
York Mahoning Mechanical Contractors, Inc.
Youngstown, OH

Electrical:
W.T. Leone's Tri-Area Electric Co., Inc.
Youngstown, OH

Chapter XI
Special Documents, Charts, Letters, Photographs and Reports

Document Section

#1 Map of Western Reserve

#2 1847 Randolph Map

#3 1847 Rootstown Map

#4 Father Boyle's Order of First Communion

#5 1900 Lenten Regulations

#6 History by Father Delmege

#7 Old Church Songs

Chart Section

#1 Population Chart of Randolph, Rootstown, Ravenna, and total in Portage County

#2 Father Delmege's chart with his explanation of the Church functions

Letter Section

#1 Father Delmege's letters to Bishop McFadden with reference to church repairs

#2 Bishop McFadden's reply to Father Delmege

#3 Father Cawley's letter referencing the building of the church hall

#4 Letter from Helen Gless to CCD teachers and parishioners

Photo Section

#1 John Carroll

#2 Edward Fenwick

#3 John Baptist Purcell

#4 Amadeus Rappe

#5 Richard Gilmour

#6 Ignatius Horstmann

#7 John Farrelly

#8 Joseph Schrembs

#9 James McFadden

#10 Emmet Walsh

#11 James Malone

#12 Thomas Tobin

#13 George Murray

#14 St. Joseph's Church, Randolph

#15 St. Peter's Church, Heppenheim, Germany

#16 1900 Majestic Altar at St. Joseph's

#17 Photo of 1926 construction of Our Lady of Lourdes shrine

#18 Driveway on the west side of St. Peter's Church, Rootstown, leading to the cemetery

#19 Iron Gate entrance to St. Peter's Cemetery, Rootstown, on the west side

#20 The drive and flowering bushes on the west side of St. Peter's Cemetery, Rootstown

#21 Life-size statue of Christ in the middle of St. Peter's Cemetery, Rootstown

#22 Life-size statue of St. Peter on the west side of St. Peter's Church, Rootstown

#23 Communion railing in dark mahogany

#24 Earlier communion railing painted white

#25 Groundbreaking for St. Peter's new hall in 1959

#26 100-Year Centennial Planning Committee

#27 100-Year Centennial Planning Committee dinner

#28 125-Year celebration dinner

#29 Construction phase of the new cemetery shrine at St. Peter's, Rootstown

#30 Finished cemetery shrine

#31 Heritage Preservation Committee

#32 Mass celebration for the new St. Peter's Church, Rootstown, on November 26, 2006

#33 1930s and 1940s Altar Rosary Society

#34 1968 Altar Rosary Society

#35 1991 Altar Rosary Society

#36 2000 Altar Rosary Society

#37 2006 Altar Rosary Society

#38 2010 Altar Rosary Society

#39 Holy Name Society 1940

#40 Later Photo of Holy Name Society

#41 1968 Traditional Choir

#42 1991 Traditional Choir

#43 1991 Contemporary Choir

#44 2000 Traditional Choir

#45 2000 Contemporary Choir

#46 2006 Traditional Choir

#47 2006 Traditional Choir

#48 2010 Contemporary Choir

#49 2010 Traditional Choir

#50 Large statue of St. Peter inside the historic church, Rootstown

#51 Large statue of St. Anthony inside the historic church, Rootstown

#52 Mary Mitsch Window

#53 Albert Mitsch Window

#54 Mrs. John Paulus Window

#55 Mr. & Mrs. Henry C. Kline Window

#56 Crucifix and Painting

#57 Sacred Heart

#58 Stations of the Cross, Historic Church

#59 Blessed Mother and St. Joseph, Historic Church

#60 Side entrances prior to 1948

#61 New Church Construction

#62 Stations of the Cross

#63 Tabernacle

#64 8' Oval Holy Spirit Window

#65 Large Crucifix

#66 Radiant Jesus

#67 Upside-down cross at end of each pew

#68 Blessed Mother Statue

#69 St. John Neumann

#70 St. Peter inside the Church

#71 St. Peter outside the Church in parking lot

#72 St. Philomena

#73 Sacred Heart with outstretched arms

#74 Book of Epistles

#75 Stanley Ambrose

#76 Charles Miley

#77 Robert Smith

#78 John Duffy

#79 Roy Paulus

#80 Donald Armbruster

#81 Robert Armbruster

#82 Ronald Armbruster

#83 Jack Miley

#84 Carl Conley

#85 Frank Cisneros

#86 Paul Marva

#87 Dennis Samblant

#88 Gerald Biltz

#89 Don Kerr

#90 Ron Albright

#91 Paul Durbak

#92 Edward Rodenbucher

#93 James Albright

#94 Eugene Muldoney

#95 Rudy Tosenberger

#96 Scott Riemenschneider

#97 Doug Palmer

<u>**Report Section**</u>

#1 Soldiers who served from Rootstown

#2 Father Lindesmith's report on original Catholic families

#3 Father Lindesmith's 1908 financial report

#4 Interview of Martin Knipp-age 100 when interviewed

#5 Report from Eloise Sweet Biltz of her recollections of Rootstown

#6 Soldiers serving from St. Peter's in WWII by Father Delmege

#7 St. Peter's Youth Group, barn dances by Joan & Marie Rice

#8 Holy Land and Crucifix painting on the wall at the front of the historic church by Mary Kline Roynesdal

#9 *The Passion Play* by Helen White (2005)

#10 A Dream Come True by Robert F. Winkler

#11 Heritage Preservation Committee report by Helen White

#12 Report/Interview of Audrey Kissell Smith

#13 List of members of miscellaneous guilds at St. Peter's

#14 *It Is Finished*

#15 The life of Saint John Nepomucene Neumann

#16 Interview of Aunts Cathryn and Julia

Document Section

Document #1
Map of Western Reserve

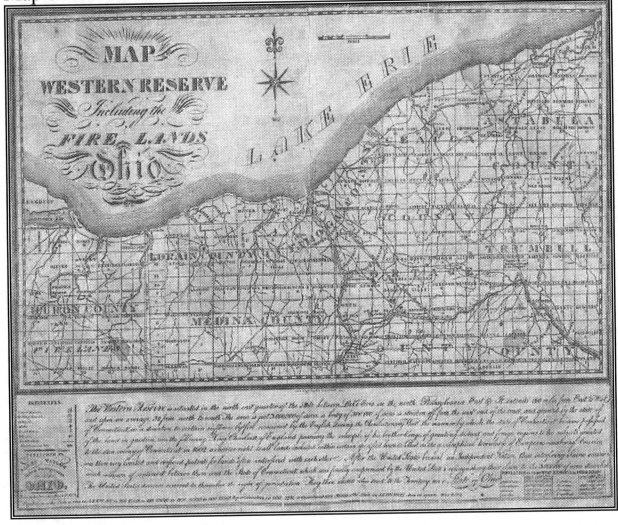

Document #2
1847 Randolph Map

Map of RANDOLPH Township
TOWN 1   RANGE 8

Document #3
1847 Rootstown Map

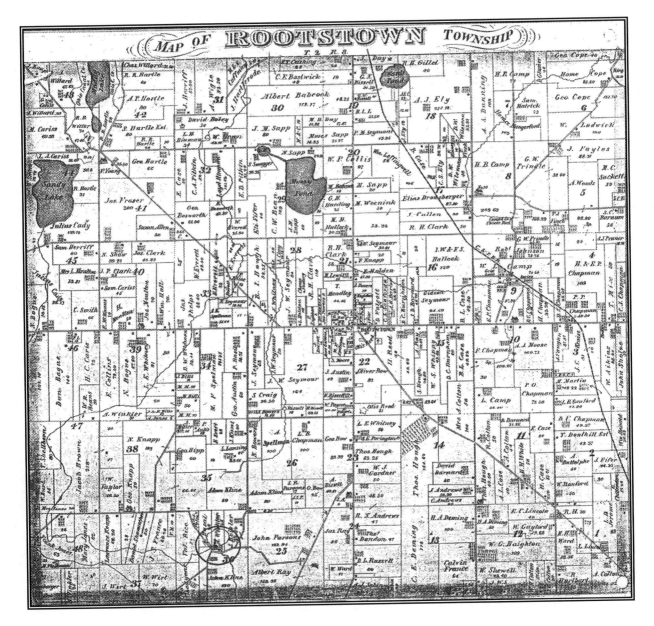

99

Document #4
Father Boyle's Order of First Communion

First Communion Day.
Afternoon Service,   Oct. 1. 1899.

1) When Priest sits down, Children sing "Litany".
2) Rosary & Litany by priest. After which the Priest sits.
3) Hymn: "Daily, daily sing to Mary", by children.
4) Investing of Children with Scapular.
5) Priest sits down, & children sing: "Mother dear, O pray for me."
6) Renewal of Bap. Promises. Children come up two by two.
7) Priest sits down, & children sing "The Priceless love of Jesus."
8) Exposition of Blessed Sacrament — Litany of S. Heart & Act of Con.
9) Regular Choir sings "O Salutaris" & "Tantum Ergo."
10) Benediction — "Gebenedeit sei Gott", etc
11) "Laudate Dominum" by Regular Choir.
12) "Grosser Gott" by all.

J.J.B.

Document #5
1900 Lenten Regulations

*These Lenten regulations have been reproduced from Father Boyle's original 1900 record book.

Ash Wednesday, the first day of Lent, falls this year on the 28th of February.

By indult of the Holy See, dated August 3, 1887, the following regulations for Lent are published for the diocese of Cleveland:

1-All the days of Lent, except Sundays, are Fast Days of Obligation.

2-All who have passed their twenty-first year, and have not begun their sixtieth, are bound to keep the fast unless legitimately dispensed.

3-All bound to keep the fast shall make but one full meal a day, except on Sunday.

4-The meal allowed on fast days is not to be taken until about noon.

5-A small refreshment, commonly called collation, is allowed in the evening. No general rule as to the quantity of food permitted at this time is or can be made. But the practice of good Catholics is, never to let it exceed the fourth part of an ordinary meal.

6-When the principal meal cannot be taken at noon, the order may be inverted and the collation can be taken at about noon and the dinner in the evening.

7-In this diocese, bread, butter, cheese, milk, eggs and all kinds of fruits, vegetables and fish are allowed at the collation.

8-By dispensation, the use of meat is allowed at any time on Sundays and once a day on Mondays, Tuesdays, Thursdays and Saturdays, with the exception of Ember Saturday (March 10) and Holy Saturday (April14).

9-On days, Sunday included, when permission is granted to eat meat, flesh and fish shall not be used at the same meal.

10-General usage has made it lawful to take in the morning a cup of coffee, tea or thin chocolate and a cracker or small piece of bread.

11-Necessity and custom have authorized the use of lard or other fat rendered from any kind of meat, instead of butter, in preparing fish, vegetables, etc.

12-The following persons are exempt from the obligation of fasting: All under twenty-one years of age, or who have begun their sixtieth year, the sick, pregnant or nursing women, those who are obliged to do hard labor; also those who through weakness cannot fast without prejudice to their health.

13-By virtue of the Indulgences granted on March 15, 1895, for ten years, by the Holy See to the Bishops in the United States, the Rt. Rev. Bishop allows working men and their families the use of flesh meat on all of the fast and abstinence days throughout the year, with the exception of all Fridays, Ash Wednesday, the Wednesday and Saturday of Holy week and the Vigil of Christmas. Those who avail themselves of this dispensation are not allowed to eat fish and meat at the same meal, and they are exhorted to perform some other acts of mortification and penance, in accord with the spirit of the Holy season of Lent. A most useful and commendable custom is that of abstaining during Lent from stimulants, in honor of the Sacred Thirst of our Divine Lord.

14-Persons dispensed from the obligation of fasting on account of age, hard labor, sickness, weak health, or any other reason, are not bound by the restriction of using meat only at one meal on days when its use is granted by dispensation. Those who are obligated to fast, are permitted to use meat only at one meal.

15-It is recommended that on Good Friday the faithful abstain from the use of milk, butter and eggs.

16-All who entertain any reasonable doubt about their obligation to fast or abstain should apply to their confessor for advice or dispensation.

To afford the faithful more abundant opportunities to gain the graces of the Lenten season, it is hereby ordered that in addition to the usual Sunday devotions, Lenten exercises be held on two evenings of each week in all churches where it is at all possible, and that after the stations of the Cross an appropriate instruction, or Benediction of the Blessed Sacrament, be given. An instruction must be given at least on one of the two evenings. One of the Lenten sermons should be on marriage.

The Good Friday offerings are devoted to the maintenance of the Holy Places in Palestine, as directed by our Holy Father, Leo XIII.

By order of the Rt. Rev. Bishop.

G.F. Houck, Chancellor.

Cleveland, O., February 21, 1900.

Document #6
History by Father Delmege
(Father's Original Report)

When the Civil War ended, Father Victor Haussner, Pastor of St. Joseph's, Randolph, was determined to build the long needed, larger Church and all its Parishioners agreed to help him. However, the families living in Rootstown Township changed their minds and decided to build a Church for themselves in their own neighborhood and thus provide a school for their children closer to their homes. So, on Dec. 31, 1866 it is recorded that: "Adam and Catherine Winkler, for $100.00, deeded to Adam Kline, Francis Gour, Martin Miller, Michael Biils and George Gouthier and their successors as Trustees of the Catholic Church in Rootstown, one acre in Lot No. 36." This property was--as it still is--between the two bridges across Breakneck Creek on The Old Forge Road. The Cemetery was officially opened with the first burial in 1867.

In 1868 the men of the congregation of the new St. Peter Parish erected a frame, Gothic style church, 30 x 45, at a cost of $1200. The building contained two rooms: one for the church itself and the other for a class room where a lay teacher would instruct the children in Religion and German. The tower was added the following year to house the new bell.

St. Peter's became a Mission of St. Joseph's, Randolph, and it remained as such for thirty years! When Father Haussner left St. Joseph's, St. Peter's was served by Father Herbstritt (1868-1891) Father Koehn (1869-1875) Father Kirch (1875-1885) Father Rebholtz (1885-1891) Father Romer (1891-1892) and Father Thein (1892-1898) until Father Boyle was appointed as his assistant and who was put in charge of St. Peter's.

The Reverend John J. Boyle, born in Philadelphia and ordained there in 1872, immediately interested the forty-five farm families in the idea of having their own Pastor. Within a short time, the church was enlarged and the Parish House built. And so, on August 1, 1899, Father Boyle became the first Resident Pastor. When he was transferred to East Palestine the following June he was succeeded for a short time by Father Timothy O'Connell and then Father Kirch returned to St. Peter's as Pastor in August 1900.

On Sept. 20, 1901, The Reverend Eli Washington John Lindesmith, seventy four years old, arrived at St. Peter's. He had already carved his name deep in the History of the Diocese and a full life time of work was behind him. He had been born in a Log Cabin in Center Township, Columbiana County, in 1827. Ordained in 1855 in Cleveland he served successively as Pastor in Doylestown, Canton, Alliance, and Leetonia. During the Sioux or "Sitting Bull" War he was appointed Chaplain in the Regular Army by President Hayes and was stationed at Fort Keough, Montana, until his discharge in 1891. Back home once more he again was sent to Doylestown from where he was transferred to St. Peter's. During his years in Rootstown where he remained until 1909 he became well known throughout Portage County for his zealous patriotism and for his many public speeches in the cause of temperance.

A protégé of Father Lindesmith's, the Reverend John P. McGoogan, followed him as Pastor. He was an accomplished musician and it was through his efforts that the men of the parish raised the church off its foundation and dug the basement for the historic church. Father McGoogan wanted a proper place where his own trained orchestra could perform. When he was sent to Warren, Father Louis LeMiller succeeded him in 1919 until Father Anthony A. Battes arrived in 1923. Then, in 1927, Dr. Siegfried A. Heyl was appointed to St. Peter's.

During the thirty years, 1868-1898, St. Peter's was a Mission of St. Joseph's, the Faith had not grown very robust and during the next thirty five years, 1898-1933, hard times, misunderstandings and other unfortunate circumstances contributed to such a loss of Parish interest on the part of the hard working farmers, that it was recommended the parish be abandoned. However, at this crucial period in the life of the Parish, the Reverend Walter J. Fowler was sent to St. Peter's by the Cleveland Auxiliary Bishop, James A. McFadden. It was a most fortunate appointment. Though not in perfect health, Father Fowler set out to remedy the ailing spiritual and material condition of the Parish. In a short time Parish interest was revived, church attendance increased, the church and rectory were repaired, the cemetery improved and enlarged. Under Father Fowler's direction, St. Peter's was reborn and began to thrive in spite of the current depression. He never spared himself in spite of his failing health until he died in St. Thomas Hospital, Akron, January 22, 1941. He is buried in the Parish Cemetery in a grave he set aside for himself.

During the illness of Father Fowler, the Reverend Robert D. Delmege was sent to St. Peter's as Administrator on December 19, 1940; he was appointed Pastor in June 1941. Many changes have come to St. Peter's during the past decade. The men and women of the Parish undertook a major improvement program which included the complete remodeling of both the interior and the exterior of the old church: a new entrance was added which included the Baptistery and Parish Library; the Sacristies were enlarged and a chapel added; the interior was redecorated and refurnished. The Parish Hall was modernized; the cemetery landscaped and, at the north end, a beautiful rustic Crucifix was erected. The Parish House was also completely remodeled. Old St. Peter's, off the beaten track, down a side road, with her scars glossed over and her hectic history behind her, sits serenely among the undulating fields of Rootstown Township, looking with confidence into the future.

Document #7
Old Church Songs

SAINT PETER'S CHURCH
Rootstown, Ohio

1.

O SALUTARIS

O Salutaris Hostia,
Quae coeli pandis ostium:
Bella premunt hostilia,
Da robur, fer auxilium.

Uni trinoque Domino
Sit sempiterna gloria!
Qui vitam sine termino
Nobis donet in patria.

TANTUM ERGO

Tantum ergo Sacramentum
Veneremur cernui:
Et antiquum documentum
Novo cedat ritui:
Praestet fides supplementum
Sensuum defectui.

Genitori, Genitoque
Laus et jubilatio.
Salus, honor, virtus quoque
Sit et benedictio:
Procedenti ab utroque
Compar sit laudatio. Amen.

V. Panem de coelo praestitisti eis.
(Alleluia.)
R. Omne delectamentum in se habentem.
(Alleluia.)

2.

HOLY GOD, WE PRAISE THY NAME

Holy God, we praise Thy name
Lord of all, we bow before Thee!
All on earth Thy sceptre claim,
All in heav'n above adore Thee.
‖:Infinite Thy vast domain,
Everlasting is Thy name.:‖ Repeat.
Hark! the loud celestial hymn,
Angel choirs above are singing,
Cherubim and Seraphim,
In unceasing chorus praising,
‖:Fill the heavens with sweet accord,
Holy! Holy! Holy Lord.:‖ Repeat.

3.

LIKE A STRONG AND RAGING FIRE

Like a strong and raging fire
In a narrow furnace pent,
Glows the Sacred Heart's desire
In the Holy Sacrament.
Round that sacred furnace thronging,
Shall these hearts refuse to burn?
Heart of love and tender longing,
Shall we make Thee no return?

Chorus—
Bending low in adoration,
While our souls are borne above,
Hear our hymn of reparation,
Heart of Jesus, be our love.

'Twas to cast abroad Love's fire,
That our God from heaven came;
May those sparks our love inspire,
May we burn with that blest flame.
All our sins, our slights, our coldness,
All our insults we deplore,
Pardon, Lord, our daring boldness,
We will never wound Thee more.

4.

JESUS, MY LORD, MY GOD, MY ALL!

Jesus, my Lord, my God, my all!
How can I love Thee as I ought?
And how revere this wondrous gift,
So far surpassing hope or thought?

Chorus—
Sweet Sacrament! we Thee adore,
O make us love Thee more and more,
O make us love Thee more and more.

Had I but Mary's sinless heart
To love Thee with, my dearest King,
O with what bursts of fervent praise
Thy goodness, Jesus, would I sing!

5.

O SACRED HEART! O LOVE DIVINE!

O Sacred Heart! O Love Divine!
Do keep us near to Thee;
And make our love so like to Thine,
That we may holy be.

Chorus—
Heart of Jesus, hear!
O Heart of Love Divine!
Listen to our prayer;
Make us always Thine.

O Temple pure! O House of gold!
Our heaven here below!
What sweet delights, what wealth untold,
From Thee do ever flow!

O Wounded Heart, O Fount of Tears!
O Throne of grief and pain!
Whereon for the eternal years,
Thy love for man does reign.

6.

TO JESUS' HEART ALL BURNING

To Jesus' Heart, all burning
With fervent love for men,
My heart with fondest yearning
Shall raise the joyful strain.

Chorus—
While ages course along,
Blest be with loudest song
The Sacred Heart of Jesus,
By every heart and tongue,
The Sacred Heart of Jesus,
By every heart and tongue.

O Heart for me on fire,
With love no man can speak,
My yet untold desire,
God gives me for Thy sake.

Too true, I have forsaken
Thy flock by willful sin;
Yet now let me taken
Back to Thy fold again.

7.

O JESUS, JESUS, DEAREST LORD

O Jesus, Jesus, dearest Lord
Forgive me if I say
For very love, Thy sacred Name,
A thousand times a day.
I love Thee so I know not how,
My transports to control,
Thy love is like a burning fire
Within my very soul.

O wonderful that Thou should'st let
So vile a heart as mine
Love Thee with such a love as this,
And make so free with Thine.
The craft of this wide world of ours
Poor wisdom seems to me;
Ah, dearest Jesus, I have grown
Childish with love of Thee.

8.

COME, HOLY GHOST, CREATOR BLEST

Come, Holy Ghost, Creator blest,
And in our hearts take up Thy rest,
Come with Thy grace and heavenly aid,
‖:To fill the hearts which Thou hast made.:‖
O Comforter! to Thee we cry;
Thou heavenly Gift of God Most High!
Thou Fount of life and Fire of love,
‖:And sweet anointing from above.:‖

9.

STABAT MATER

1.
Weeping sore, the Mother stood
Nigh the Cross, the fatal wood
Whereon hung her dying Son.

2.
Through her soul for anguish crying,
Sunk in sorrow, spent with sighing,
The prophetic sword had run.

3.
Oh, how sad, how heavy laden,
Was that meek and blessed Maiden,
God's true Mother undefiled.

4.
Trembling, grieving, whelmed in woes,
When she saw the dying throes
Of her own immortal Child.

5.
Who is he whose weeping eyes,
Would not choose but sympathize
With the Mother of our Lord.

6.
Who is he that would refuse
Pity for such Mother's woes,
Weeping o'er her Son adored.

7.
Tortured for His sinful race,
She beheld each ghastly trace
Of His scourging at the post.

8.
She beheld her Son so sweet
Dying and all desolate
When He yielded up the Ghost.

9.
Come, dear Mother, love's sweet spring,
Let me share thy sorrowing,
Let my tears unite with thine.

10.
Let my heart be wrapt in fire,
Still to seek with fond desire,
Christ, my God, my love Divine.

11.
Holy Mother, this impart,
Deeply print upon my heart,
All the wounds He dying bore.

12.
Let me share His pains with thee,
Who so tenderly for me
Deigned those sorrows to endure.

13.
Let our tears in one same tide
Flow for Jesus crucified,
Long as life shall warm my breast.

14.
By the Cross to take my station,
Share thy tender lamentation,
This is my most fond request.

15.
Brightest of the Virgin train,
Do not thou my suit disdain,
Let me share thy grief with thee.

10.

MOTHER DEAREST, MOTHER FAIREST

Mother dearest, Mother fairest,
　Help of all who call on thee,
Virgin purest, brightest, rarest,
　Help us, help, we cry to thee.

Chorus—

　‖:Mary, help us, help we pray,:‖
　　Help us in all care and sorrow;
　Mary, help us, help we pray.

Lady, help in pain and sorrow,
　Soothe those rack'd on bed of pain;
May the golden light of morrow
　Bring them health and joy again.

11.

MOTHER DEAR, O PRAY FOR ME!

Mother dear, O pray for me!
　Whilst far from Heav'n and thee,
I wander in a fragile bark,
　O'er life's tempestuous sea;
O Virgin Mother, from thy throne,
　So bright in bliss above,
Protect thy child and cheer my path,
　With thy sweet smile of love.

Chorus—

　Mother dear, remember me,
　　And never cease thy care,
　'Till in heaven eternally,
　　Thy love and bliss I share.

Mother dear, O pray for me!
　Should pleasure's siren lay
E'er tempt thy child to wander far
　From virtue's path away;
When thorns beset life's devious way,
　And darkling waters flow,
Then Mary, aid thy weeping child,
　Thyself a mother show.

12.

AVE MARIA! BRIGHT AND PURE

Ave Maria! bright and pure,
　Hear, O hear me when I pray;
Pains and pleasures try the pilgrim
　On his long and dreary way.
Fears and perils are around me,
　Ave Maria, bright and pure,
　Ora pro me, Ora pro me.

Ave Maria, Queen of heav'n,
　Teach, O teach me to obey;
Lead me on through fierce temptations,
　Stand and meet me in the way.
When I fail and faint, my Mother,
　Ave Maria, bright and pure,
　Ora pro me, Ora pro me.

13.

ON THIS DAY, O BEAUTIFUL MOTHER

Chorus—

On this day, O beautiful Mother,
　On this day we give thee our love.
Near thee, Madonna, fondly we hover,
　Trusting thy gentle care to prove.

On this day we ask to share,
　Dearest Mother, thy sweet care;
Aid us ere our feet astray
　Wander from thy guiding way.
　　　　　　　　—Chorus.

Queen of angels deign to hear
　Lisping children's humble pray'r;
Young hearts gain, O Virgin pure,
　Sweetly to thyself allure.
　　　　　　　　—Chorus.

14.

MARY, DEAREST MOTHER

Mary, dearest Mother,
　From thy heavenly height
Look on us thy children,
　Lost in earth's dark night.

Chorus—

　Oh! we pray thee, loved Mary,
　　Mary, fondly we entreat,
　Guide us to our sweet Saviour,
　　And leave us at His feet;
　Mary, shield us from danger,
　　Keep our souls from sin,
　Help thy exiled children,
　　Heav'n at last to win.

Oh! we love thee, Mary,
　Trusting all to thee;
What is past or present,
　What is yet to be.

Mother of our Saviour,
　Hear our pleading prayer,
Take us 'neath thy mantle,
　Hide, oh, hide us there.

15.

MOTHER OF CHRIST

Mother of Christ, Mother of Christ,
　What shall I ask of thee?
I do not sigh for wealth of earth,
　For joys that fade and flee.
But, Mother of Christ, Mother of Christ,
　This do I long to see,
The bliss untold, which thine arms enfold,
　The treasure upon thy knee.

Mother of Christ, Mother of Christ,
　He's all in all to thee,
In winter's cave, in Naz'reth's home,
　In the hamlets of Galilee;
So, Mother of Christ, Mother of Christ,
　He'll not say nay to thee,
When He lifts His face to thy sweet
　embrace.
O speak to Him, Mother, of me.

16.

GOOD NIGHT, SWEET JESUS

Good night, sweet Jesus, guard us in sleep,
Our souls and bodies in Thy love keep
Waking or sleeping, keep us in sight,
Dear, gentle Saviour, good night, good
　night.
Good night, dear Jesus, good night, good
　night.

Good night, sweet Jesus, grant that each
　day
Of our lives mortal, thus pass away,
Thy love e'er watching, guiding aright,
Dear, gentle Saviour, good night, good
　night.
Good night, dear Jesus, good night, good
　night.

17.

JESUS, SAVIOUR OF MY SOUL

Jesus! Saviour of my soul,
　Let me to Thy refuge fly,
While the nearer waters roll,
　While the tempest still is nigh.

Chorus—

　Hide me, O my Saviour, hide
　　Till the storm of life is past
　Safe into Thy haven guide
　　O receive my soul at last.

Jesus Saviour of my soul
　Let me to Thy refuge fly;
Ave, Ave, Jesus mild,
　Deign to hear Thy lowly child.

18.

WILT THOU LOOK UPON ME, MOTHER

Wilt thou look upon me, Mother,
　Thou who reignest in the skies,
Wilt thou deign to cast upon me
　One sweet glance from those mild eyes.

Chorus—

Oh, my Mother Mary, still remember
　What the sainted Bernard said,
None have ever, ever found thee wanting
　‖:Who have called upon thy aid.:‖

Wilt thou, Mother, hover ever
　On my pathway still to guide,
Wilt thou whisper kind directions
　To the angel by my side?

19.

O LORD, I AM NOT WORTHY

O Lord, I am not worthy
　That Thou shouldst come to me,
But speak the words of comfort,
　My spirit healed shall be.

And humbly I'll receive Thee
　The Bridegroom of my soul,
No more by sin to grieve Thee,
　Or fly Thy sweet control.

Yes, dear Jesus, I believe it
　And Thy presence I adore,
And with all my heart I love Thee
　May I love Thee more and more.

O Sacrament most holy
O Sacrament divine,
All praise and all thanksgiving
Be every moment Thine.

20.

SWEET SAVIOUR! BLESS US

Sweet Saviour! bless us ere we go,
　Thy word into our minds instill;
And make our lukewarm hearts to glow
　With lowly love and fervent will.

Chorus—

　Through life's long day, and death's
　　dark night,
　　O gentle Jesus, be our light,
　　O gentle Jesus, be our light.

The day is done, its hour has run;
　And Thou hast taken count of all;
The scanty triumphs grace hath won,
　The broken vow, the frequent fall.

21.

BRING FLOWERS OF THE RAREST

Bring flowers of the rarest, bring flowers
　of the fairest,
From garden and woodland, and hillside
　and vale;
Our full hearts are swelling, our glad voices
　telling
The praise of the loveliest Rose of the dell.

Chorus—

‖:Oh Mary! we crown thee with blossoms
　today,
Queen of the Angels, Queen of the May.:‖

Our voices ascending, in harmony blending,
Oh! thus may our hearts turn, dear Mother,
　to thee;
Oh! thus shall we prove thee how truly
　we love thee,
How dark without Mary, life's journey
　would be.

Chart Section

Chart #1
Population Chart of Randolph, Rootstown, Ravenna, and total in Portage County

Year	Randolph	Rootstown	Ravenna	Portage County
1802	6	6		
1810	165			2,995
1820	328			6,531
1830	690		806	
1840	1,649			22,965
1850	1,732	1,308		24,419
1860	1,686	1,283	2,849	24,208
1870	1,564	1,169		24,584
1880	1,684	1,217		27,500
1890	1,492			27,868
1900	1,389			29,246
1910	1,345			30,307
1920	1,376			36,269
1930	1,733			42,682
1940	1,899			46,660
1950	2,302			63,954
1960	2,949	3,831		91,798
1970	4,150	6,010		125,868
1980	5,093	6,585		135,856
1990	4,970	6,612		142,585
2000	5,504	7,212		152,061

*A devastating fire in 1854 destroyed most of the Johnny Cake Hollow settlement. Note the decline of population after that date.

Note: Population of Portage County in 2010, approximately 186,000 people.

Chart #2

Father Delmege's chart with his explanation of the Church functions.

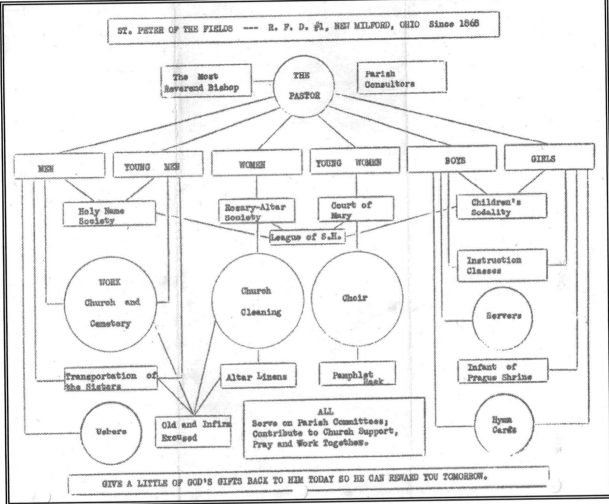

ST. PETER OF THE FIELDS

(ROOTSTOWN TOWNSHIP)

SINCE 1868

SUNDAY MASSES
8:00 - 10:00

P. O. ADDRESS RFD No. 1
NEW MILFORD, OHIO

August 1, 1945

Dear Parishioner:

　　　　1) The enclosed Diagram is not a puzzle though it may look like one at first glance. It is a Diagram showing the various Parish activities for every man, woman and child of St. Peter's. The Most Reverend Bishop is the Head of the Diocese, the Pastor is the Head of the Parish and YOU are the important members. If you are a man follow the lines from the block "Men" and you will see what you are expected to do for the welfare of your Parish, etc. If YOU as an individual fail to cooperate in the activities outlined for you then you are a burden to all the other members. Ask yourself after studying this diagram if you and members of your family have been lending your presence and assistance to every part of the Parish Program. Whenever you are asked to do something --anything--for the welfare of your Parish consider it a duty and a privilege! When you renege, chisel, cheat, --- you are not the only one to suffer!

　　　　2) Also enclosed is an envelope for you and members of your household.....envelopes for your contributions toward the 1945 Annual Summer Campaign. Do you ever reflect that it costs about $350.00 each and every month of the year to operate your Parish? Reflect that the Sunday Offertory does not come near meeting this monthly expense? Your Pew Rent, Socials and this Summer Campaign must make up the deficit and what is over is put into the Church Remodeling Fund.

　　　　3) Last year we added to the Fund but IT HAS BEEN NECESSARY TO USE SOME OF THIS MONEY BECAUSE OF EXTRA EXPENSES! Not only is it costing more to operate the Parish but REPAIRING THE CHURCH ROOF AND THE REPAIR OF THE EXPLOSION DAMAGE IN THE PARISH HOUSE cost nearly $600.00! Hence, knowing your interest in the Parish and knowing your generosity, make an effort to give more in the Summer Campaign than last year! Consult the list on the Bulletin Board -- it lists your donation of 1944. Remember too a wage earner that gives but $5.00 gives in actual value but $3.94½! There are a few who can give no more than this and God bless them for their good will. "Give while you live!"

　　　　With many thanks to those fine men and women who have constantly co-operated with me, your Pastor, in every effort and wishing each and all bountiful graces, I am

　　　　Sincerely yours in Christ,

　　　　F. Dehnega

St. Peter of the Fields
R. F. D. No. 1.
NEW MILFORD, O.

108

Letter Section

Letter #1
Father Delmege's letters to Bishop McFadden with reference to church repairs.

ST. PETER'S OF THE FIELDS

ROOTSTOWN TOWNSHIP

SUNDAY
MASSES:
8:00
10:00

October 23, 1943

The Most Reverend James A. McFadden, S.T.D.,
Diocese of Youngstown, 144 West Wood Street,
Youngstown, Ohio.

P. O. Address
R. D. 1
New Milford, Ohio

Dear Bishop McFadden:

Because our Church roof needs attention I would like your decision on an important matter: When Bishop Hoban was here for Confirmation he said that I should be content with making but the most necessary repairs because the Church should be located in Rootstown Center. Of course there are reasons why it ought to be there and, probably, many reasons why it should remain here.

When the house was reconditioned it was done not only because it needed it but also because if the Church was to be relocated the house could be sold or rented. The Cemetery received constant attention because that will always remain. The Church floor supports were replaced because, according to Mr Koehl, there was grave danger of the whole thing collapsing. But nothing else has been done on the Church. Now we would like to begin the repairing and remodeling of it so, finally, it could be decorated; it has not been painted since about 1921.

But if you think the Church should be relocated in Rootstown Center then I'll rest content to repair the roof and not replace it as should be done for permanent use; if the Church should remain here of course we'll do a more lasting job. It was my intention to begin the remodeling in Spring when the necessary labor was promised but remembering Bishop Hoban's advice I would appreciate a word from you now. If you believe we ought to relocate in Rootstown I think that decision should be made at this time before an unnecessary dollar is spent.

If you wish to discuss this problem a little more in detail I will be pleased to come to your office whenever you suggest a convenient time for you and will bring whatever information about the place you would like.

With kindest personal regards, I am

Respectfully yours,

B. J. X. Delmege

Letter #2
Bishop McFadden's reply to Father Delmege.

October 26, 1943

The Reverend Robert D. Delmedge,   Pastor,
St. Peter's of the Fields
Rootstown, R.D. # 1,
New Milford, Ohio.

Dear Father Delmedge:

        I feel that you should proceed
at once to repair the roof of the Church, and begin the
remodeling of the Church and make its interior
beautiful and worthy of our Blessed Lord and of the
good parishioners who made so many sacrifices. I am
very proud of what has been done in this parish for
the Faith.   The last fifteen years have been most
inspiring.

        There is no need at present to
consider a change of site. There are so many beautiful
memories with St. Peter of the Fields. A change of
site would take away that name. You tell your good
people, that I desire to see the Church made beautiful
by you who have have such a fine appreciation of the
artistic and the liturgical. I know that they will
help. I want you to express my admiration for what
they have done.

            Yours devotedly in Christ,

JAMcF.AAP.   Bishop of Youngstown

Letter #3
Father Cawley's letter referencing the building of the church hall.

St. Peter of the Fields
RD#2 New Milford, Ohio

August 18, 1959

Dear Parishioner,

I have been told repeatedly by Parishioners that we need a Hall here - and soon. So we have finally decided to make a move. However, I want no part of it unless 100% of our people are behind it. Last week we sent a letter saying this - and it was time for the Annual Summer Campaign anyway (you have had this for years - it was only dropped while the Cathedral Drive lasted). However, this year we suggested no particular amount - but especially asked for a yes or no re plans for expansion. The letter, the Gleanings and the sermon last Sunday made this clear.

So that you will have a fuller picture of the situation, this letter should help. We need a Hall because:
1. A priest can only say two Masses on Sundays - except in very special cases. The addition of the third Mass was a great help. A Paraclet priest says one Mass in St. Joseph's and one here. This is only a temporary arrangement. There is no way of adding a fourth Mass.
2. Rather than tear down the present church and build one adequate for our needs, we need the Hall. (A new church would cost $150,000).
3. The present church would be used for everything except one Mass on Sundays. Such a plan would fulfill our needs for years.
4. If you ever build a school - and it looks like you will have to some day - you need an auditorium.
5. Bingo income would be more than doubled.
6. We would have a decent place for Catechism classes and C.Y.O. activities.
7. We would have the finest Hall in the area - for dinners, conventions, weddings, etc.

If we get enough of yes answers, we will call a meeting of all our people on Monday, August 31st, and everyone can say his piece. At the meeting we would form a Building Committee and decide re size and location of Hall, etc., and devise ways and means of placing a fair share of the cost on each family.

We would need a building (facing the road) about 125 feet long and 50 feet wide, with full glazed tile basement. The basement could contain the heating system, toilets and space for all sorts of storage. In the upstairs, we could have a stage, to be also used for an altar, with two side sacristys. The main body of the building would seat about 600. There would be no posts, and the walls should have glazed tile about five feet high. A contractor friend has told me such a building could be put up for about $20,000.

The above information should be of help to you. Your parish is at a crossroads. Where there is a will, there is a way. A few hours wages a month from everybody would pay for this Building over about two years. You pay that amount for insurance every year. What about Eternal-life Insurance? Jesus Christ, His Mother, and St. Peter will remember you.

Many thanks for your kind co-operation with my efforts for the advancement of St. Peter of the Fields.

Sincerely,

Father Cawley

FATHER GERARD CAWLEY
and Councilmen

Letter #4
Letter from Helen Gless to CCD teachers and parishioners

December 1968

Dear St. Peter of the Fields
    C. C. D. Friends:

As the shining eyes of
"our" children reflect the joy,
happiness and hope we all
share at this time of year —
we extend to you our heartfelt
appreciation and our sincere
good wishes!

May your holiday be bright
with joy and may the coming
year be blessed with good
health and good fortune for
those you love!

During this season of
sharing we ask that a
contribution be placed in the
Sunday collection marked "C.C.D.
Gift" for Father Gawron and the
Notre Dame Sisters who enrich
our "C. C. D. Program."

Please remember to thank
our C.C.D. Lay Teachers and
offer prayers to the Holy
Spirit to guide us in this
very important work!

there will not be any
C.C.D. Classes until January 5
1969. Merry Christmas and
a Happy New Year!

God Bless You
    Mrs. Gless,
    C. C. D. Staff

112

Photo Section

List of Bishops followed by their photos
(photos #1-13 are of the Bishops)
      On April 29, 1789, George Washington became the first president of the United States of America. He was a close and personal friend of John Carroll. On November 6, 1789, Pope Pius VI named John Carroll the first Bishop of Baltimore with jurisdiction over all Catholics in the new republic of the United States of America.

Cincinnati Diocese Established 1821

Bishop Edward Fenwick	1821-1832
Bishop John Paptist Purcell	1833-1883
Bishop John Carroll	

Cleveland Diocese Established 1847

Bishop Amadeus Rappe	1847-1870
Bishop Richard Gilmour	1872-1891
Bishop Ignatius Horstmann	1892-1908
Bishop John Farrelly	1909-1921
Bishop Joseph Schrembs	1921-1943

Youngstown Diocese Established 1943

Bishop James A. McFadden	1943-1952
Bishop Emmet M. Walsh	1952-1968
Bishop James W. Malone	1968-1995
Bishop Thomas J. Tobin	1996-2005
Bishop George V. Murry	2007-To Date

Photo #1 John Carroll

Photo #5 Richard Gilmour

Photo #2 Edward Fenwick

Photo #3 John Baptist Purcell

Photo #6 Ignatius Horstmann

Photo #4 Amadeus Rappe

Photo #7 John Farrelly

Photo #8 Joseph Schrembs

Photo #9 James McFadden

Photo #10 Emmet Walsh

Photo #11 James Malone

Photo #12 Thomas Tobin

Photo #13 George Murray

Photo #14
St. Joseph's Church, Randolph

Photo #17 Photo of 1926 construction of Our Lady of Lourdes shrine

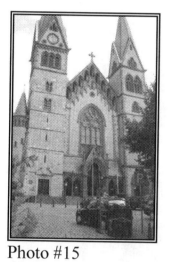

Photo #15
St. Peter's Church, Heppenheim, Germany

Photo #18 Driveway on the west side of St. Peter's Church, Rootstown, leading to the cemetery

Photo #16 1900 Majestic Altar at St. Joseph's

Photo #19 Iron Gate entrance to St. Peter's Cemetery, Rootstown, on the west side

Photo #20 The drive and flowering bushes on the west side of St. Peter's Cemetery, Rootstown

Photo #22 Life-size statue of St. Peter on the west side of St. Peter's Church, Rootstown

Photo #21 Life-size statue of Christ in the middle of St. Peter's Cemetery, Rootstown

Photo #23 Communion railing in dark mahogany

Photo #24 Earlier communion railing painted white

Photo #27 100-Year Centennial Planning Committee dinner

Far left, back row: John Adam, William Luli, David Knapp holding baby David Knapp, George Luli Sr., Father Gerald Cawley (center), Jack Miley, John Rodenbucher, Ray Knapp, Ron Knapp, far right: Ray Kline, left front: Roy Kline, young boy: Richard Knapp, two boys either side of Father Cawley unknown.

Photo #25 Groundbreaking for St. Peter's new hall in 1959

Photo #28 125-Year celebration dinner

Photo #26 100-Year Centennial Planning Committee

Photo #29 Construction phase of the new cemetery shrine at St. Peter's, Rootstown

Photo #30 Finished cemetery shrine

Photo #33 1930s and 1940s Altar Rosary Society

Photo #31 Heritage Preservation Committee

Photo #34 1968 Altar Rosary Society

Photo #32 Mass celebration for the new St. Peter's Church, Rootstown, on November 26, 2006

Photo #35 1991 Altar Rosary Society

Photo #36 2000 Altar Rosary Society

Photo #37/38 2006/2010 Altar Rosary
Society

Photo #39 Holy Name Society 1940

53 Men Enroll At Rootstown

ROOTSTOWN—With hands uplifted, 53 men of St. Peter Parish took the Holy Name pledge Easter Sunday afternoon and were received into the Holy Name Society. The pledge was administered by the Rev. Robert D. Delmege, in charge of the parish.

After the solemn reception, Ernest Paulus was elected president; Joseph Leyland, vice president, Joseph Knoch, secretary and Louis Biltz, treasurer.

Others members received were: John Angebrandt Sr., John Angebrandt Jr., Charles Biltz, Rudolph Biltz, Charles Bildershein, George Bildershein, Mike Bildershein Jr., Fred Bolanz, Clem Eichler, William Engelhart, Marion Esposito, Gaetano Esposito, Loius Esposito, Albert Esposito, John Hieber, William Heisler, John Horning, Cletus Kline, George Kline, Gus Kline, Harold Kline, Sylvan Kline, Oliver Knapp, Paul Knapp, Oscar Knapp, Francis Knoch, Bernard Lampe, William Lansinger, Harry Leyland, Jack Leyland, George Luli, Joseph Luli, Robert Luli, Dan Lynch, Toby Magos Sr., Toby Magos Jr., Charles Miley, Perry Moledor, Robert Moledor, Adam Moskal, Paul Moskal, Joseph Polack, Andrew Polack Jr., Paul Riedinger, John Rodenbucher, William Shrader, Ben Thompson Sr., John Winkler I and John Winkler II.

1st row: Louis Biltz, John Duffy, Harry Leyland, John Angebrandt, Fr. Robert Delmege, John Kropac, Adam Gungle, Mick Calabria, Richard Biltz, Marion Esposito, John Rodenbucher.
2nd row: Louis Esposito, Glen Smith, Roy Kline, Ernest Paulus, Kenneth Smith, George Bildershein, Mike Bildershein, John Trares, Ray Rodenbucher, Ray Kline.
3rd row: Oscar Knapp, Robert Kaltenbach, John Hieber, Francis Knoch, Phil Smith, William Kline.
4th row: Charles Miley, Clem Eichler, George Luli, John Benich, John Slimak, Joe Rodenbucher, Edward Bildershein, Harold Kline.

Photo #40 Holy Name Society 1950

Photo #41 1968 Traditional Choir

Photo #42 1991 Traditional Choir

Photo #43 1991 Contemporary Choir

Photo #46 2006 Traditional Choir

Photo #44 2000 Traditional Choir

Photo #47 2006 Traditional Choir

Photo #45 2000 Contemporary Choir

Photo #48 2010 Contemporary Choir

Photo #49 2010 Traditional Choir

Photo #51 Large statue of St. Anthony inside the historic church, Rootstown

Photo #50 Large statue of St. Peter inside the historic church, Rootstown

Photo #52 Mary Mitsch Window

Photo #53 Albert Mitsch Window

Photo #55
Mr. & Mrs. Henry C. Kline Window

Photo #54 Mrs. John Paulus Window

Photo #56 Crucifix and Painting

Photo #57 Sacred Heart

Photo #59 Blessed Mother and St. Joseph, Historic Church

Photo #60 Side entrances prior to 1948

Photo #58 Stations of the Cross, Historic Church

Addition to photo #61 next page

Photo #61 New Church Construction

Photo #63 Tabernacle

Photo #62 Stations of the Cross

Photo #64 8' Oval Holy Spirit Window

Photo # 63 enlarged

Photo #65 Large Crucifix

Photo #66 Radiant Jesus

Photo #68 Blessed Mother Statue

Photo #67 Upside-down cross at end of each pew

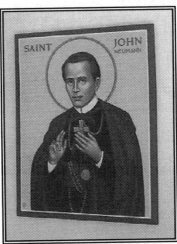

Photo #69 St. John Neumann

Photo #70 St. Peter inside the Church

Photo #72 St. Philomena

Photo #71 St. Peter outside the Church in parking lot

Photo #73 Sacred Heart with outstretched arms

Photo #74 Book of Epistles

Photo #77 Robert Smith

Photo #75 Stanley Ambrose

Photo #78 John Duffy

Photo #76 Charles Miley

Photo #79 Roy Paulus

Photo #80 Donald Armbruster

Photo #83 Jack Miley

Photo #81 Robert Armbruster

Photo #84 Carl Conley

Photo #82 Ronald Armbruster

Photo #85 Frank Cisneros

Photo #86 Paul Marva

Photo #89 Don Kerr

Photo #87 Dennis Samblant

Photo #90 Ron Albright

Photo #88 Gerald Biltz

Photo #91 Paul Durbak

Photo #92 Edward Rodenbucher

Photo #95 Rudy Tosenberger

Photo #93 James Albright

Photo #96 Scott Riemenschneider

Photo #94 Eugene Muldoney

Photo #97 Doug Palmer

Report Section

Report #1
Soldiers who served from Rootstown
As Referred to in Chapter I

War of 1812—June 1812 to December 1814:

Amidon, Abiram
Bartlett, Samuel
Campbell, John
Caris, John

Hartle, Samuel
Maxfield, William
Newberry, Chauncy
Root, Henry

Turner, John
Tuthill, Samuel
Willyard, Phillip
Wright, John

Mexican War— May 1846 to February 1848

Adam Winkler

Civil War—April 1861 to April 1865:

Andrews, Clinton
Andrews, William
Austin, James
Barnard, C.E.
Basil, John
Bissell, George
Bissell, D.R.
Belding, W.P
Bow, C.J.
Bean, John
Bean, William
Clark, A.G.
Clark, V.A.
Chapman, J.E.
Campbell, Albert
Coffin, Frederick
Deming, H.A.
Deming, W.J.
Ensign, H.L.
Englehart, Peter
Ely, Caleb

Foster, James
Gillet, Wm. Jr.
Gardener, I.W.
Geylin, George
Goss, Warren
Gibbons, Wm. S
Hinman, Lloyd
Hallock, I.W.
Hallock, E.S.
Hazen, J.A.
Heriff, Henry
Heriff, Ira
Heighton, Thomas
Harsh, Frank
Holcomb, Albert
Huffman, George
Keller, Casper
King, Miles
Kissell, John
Munroe, C.R.
Munroe, George

Northrop, E.C.
Norton, Theodore D.
Parsons, John S.
Purrington, E.C.
Ray, Alexander
Reed, S.S.
Reed, G.P.
Reed, H.L.
Sanford, L.R.
Sperra, Ezra
Spelman, A.M.
Seymour, J.M.
Tuttle, M.E.
Vaughn, Willard
Wells, J.A.
Wildman, John
Whitney, O.E.
Whitney, N.H.
Whitney, C.M.
Richardson, H.B.
Smith, Joseph

Spanish-American War—April 1898 to December 1898:

Bow, Charlie

World War I—April 1917 to November 1918:

Armitage, Chester G.
Armitage, H. Vaughn
Benshoff, Carl
Babcock, George C.
Beyers, Fay
Biltz, Robert
Bosko, Peter Wm.
Bower, Clarence
Bower, William
Brown, Grover
Coffman, Carl
College, George D.
Conaway, Charles
Corany, Dominic
Day, Charles F.
Doreflinger, Will

Dundon, Arthur
Dundon, Merle
Evans, Andy
Gauer, Joe
Gibson, Wilbert B.
Gilmore, Harley
Gombert, Louis
Hallock, Gibbs
Hartung, Edward W.
Kazimer, John J.
Kibler, Charlie
Kline, Erwin
Kline, Gust
Leadbetter, Clarence D.
Leavingood, Paul
Lindsey, Robert

Luli, Floyd A.
McNulty, Earl
Mitchell, Clayton
Mittendorf, Charlie
Moinet, Charley
Parham, John
Peairs, Alvin A.
Peairs, John
Schinke, Walter R.
Schinke, William
Smith, Craig
Smith, Silas
Stajancha, Joe
Varney, Leon
Yost, ?

World War II—December 1941 to September 1945:

Adair, Clifford
Adams, Harvey
Anderson, Edward
Anderson, Floyd
Anderson, Wilbur
Anderson, William
Angebrandt, John
Armitage, Russell
Armitage, Willard
Armstrong, Richard
Arnold, Dorsey
Arnold, Robert
Barlow, Loron
Bauer, Richard
Baumgartner, Joe
Bean, Carl
Beasley, James
Beaumont, Glenn
Beck, Richard
Beck, William
Bendar, George
Bennett, Charles

Benshoff, Robert
Benshoff, Stanley
Benson, Ray
Berry, Dorwin
Berry, Harold
Bildershein, Charles
Bildershein, Mike
Biltz, Carl
Blair, Phillip
Bloom, Clarence
Boling, Maynard
Boling, Ray
Bowland, Leonard
Bradley, Derwin
Britton, Garland
Brown, Robert
Buirley, Francis
Buirley, Robert
Church, Ralph
Chudenov, Mike
Clark, Ray
Conley, Leroy

Davis, Walter
De Hart, Virgil
De Vault, William
Dibble, Marsh
Dunlap, Frederick
Dunlap, Charles
Esposito, Albert
Esposito, Louis
Friedoff, Robert
Galloway, Homer
Geib, Fred
Gerren, Robert
Gerren, Wallace
Giordenango, Anthony
Giordenango, Charles
Girton, Preston
Girton, Wallace
Grega, Andrew
Grega, Joe
Grega, Paul
Grega, Steve
Grund, Earl

Hamilton, Russell
Harris, Robert
Hartung, Harold
Hartung, Ray
Heritage, Albert
Hluch, Joe
Jones, Sam
Kelley, Ernest
Kirby, Harold
Kline, Harold
Knapp, Paul
Krizo, John
Krogi, Andy
Krogi, John
Laubert, Forrest
Laubert, Harold
Lee, William
Leedom, James
Leedom, Ralph
Leyland, Jack
Loomis, Richard
Loomis, Robert
Lucas, Robert
Marks, Calvin
McElhiney, Wesley
Marshall, Max
Marshall, Ray
Marshall, Wilbur
Melroy, Gordon
Miley, Charles
Miller, Clifford
Miller, Dean
Miller, Floyd

Miller, Marjorie
Miller, Robert
Mitchell, Everett
Mlasofsky, John
Moser, Warren
Murray, Claude
Ney, Charles
Nichols, George
Nichols, Robert
Noel, Richard L.
Parks, Joe
Parsons, Joe
Pfile, Donald
Phillips, Robert
Polack, Andrew
Polack, Joseph
Reiss, Donald
Reiss, Kenneth
Reynolds, Art
Reynolds, Kermit
Roberto, Angelo
Robertson, Ernest
Rodocher, Dwight
Rouse, Paul
Royer, Alfred
Russell, Marlin
Saburon, Edward
Sekulich, Edward
Seymour, Deming
Sharp, James
Sheffield, Fred
Shrigley, James
Slater, Kenneth

Slater, George
Slater, Ray
Smith, John A.
Smith, Marvin
Snyder, Ervin
Staley, Willard
Stefancik, William
Stephens, Nelson
Stephenson, Paul
Straton, Garland
Straton, Henrey
Thomas, Bill
Troxel, Bob
Twiggs, Harley
Ulm, Burdette
Wancik, Steve
Ward, Gerald
Ward, Richard
Weaver, Edward
Weinkauf, Chris
Weinkauf, Howard
Weinkof, Louis
White, Roy
Williams, Norman
Wise, James
Wise, Richard
Wolford, French
Wolford, Harold
Wolford, Merrill
Wolford, Ruhl
Woodring, Wilson

After WWII, Service Men and Women Included:

Ott Allen, Don Bull, Frank Bildershein, Anthony Calabria, Edward Capela, Bob Cheatwood, Duane Craig, Frank Darsh, Roger Duke, Don Echnat, Joe Esposito, Don Gauer, Jim Gerren, Chas. Hall, Jas. Harmon, Laurence Harrell, Robt. Hylbert, Carl Jacobs, Chris Jacobs, Jack Jacobs, Helen Jordon, Joe Kerr, Mike Korval, John Kropac, Paul Long, Wm. Luli, Gary Michael, Don Moulton, Enlow Murray, Teddy Reusch, Paul Reimenschneider, Ray Rodenbucher, Rita Rodenbucher, Fred Sheffield, Wilbur Sheffield, Jas. Skeen, Paul Stephenson, Robt. Stephenson, Mike Vartanian, Peter Wahn, Roland Ward, Howard Whitted, Dick Wilson, Thos. Wilson, Ralph

Shrigley, Robert Armbruster, Robert F. Winkler, John Winkler, Robert J. Winkler, Edward Rodenbucher, & James Winkler.

This is but a partial list of those who served in the military after WWII. A complete list could not be located in Portage County records.

Report #2
Father Lindesmith's report on original Catholic families

Some of Father Lindesmith's sentence structures are not grammatically correct. His report was left that way to preserve Father's original typing.

Aug 24, 1902

THE CATHOLIC CHURCH by Rev. Father E.J. Lindesmith. St. Peter's Catholic Church between the two bridges on Breakneck Creek, Rootstown Township, Portage County, Ohio.

The original Catholics came here in 1832. Nearly all came before 1842, a few more came before 1856. They were anxious to be citizens and as soon as the law permitted, took out their naturalization papers, that is swore allegiance, support and loyalty to their adopted country and the Stars and Stripes. They immediately bought land, built homes where the third generation is now living. The original settlers all came from the following villages; Bierstat, Hemspach, Sunnabach, Keschhanse, Darmstst, Prussia, of the Palaatinate Germany. Eppemhrim, Erbach, Charles Haszinger and wife Katherine Berg arrived Sept. 16, 1832. They lived where Margaret Adam Winkler now resides. She died Oct. 29, 1851 he died Feb. 10, 1868; their children , Katherine was married and resides in Archard, Mitchell County, Ia., Elizabeth married Frank Gauer April 20, 1858.

John Gauer and wife Margaret Riez arrived in 1832. Their children; John, Charles, Frank, Valentine, Bartholomew and Katherine.

John Heisler and wife Barbara Eck, came in 1832. Children; John, Katherine, Adam, Joseph, Elizabeth, Barbara, George, Henry, Charles and Martin.

Peter Knapp and wife Elizabeth came in 1835. Children; Elizabeth, Barbara, Margaret, Susan, Phillip and John.

Adam Schweigert and wife Catherine Winkler came in 1840. Adopted nephew Adam Winkler, who in 1846 volunteered and went to the Mexican War. He married Katherine Gauer Oct. 8, 1850. Children were, John, Valentine, Catherine, Frank, Elizabeth, Margaret and Charles. He married his second wife Mary Zimer, Oct. 12, 1876; one child, Katherine. He married his third wife, Margaret Rose Rietinger Oct. 7, 1882.

Adam Kline and wife Barbara Knapp settled here in 1839. Children; Elizabeth, Barbara, Margaret, Mary, Adam, Henry, John B., George and two died in infancy.

Phillip Miller and wife Elizabeth Ardolph came in 1841. Children; Katherine, Anna, Narla, Elizabeth and John.

Nicholas Knapp and wife Anna Mary Neff, came in 1846. Children George, John, Lawrence, Nicholas, Adam and Mary.

Martin Miller came in 1840 and married Eva Reis. Child, Eva. Married second wife Barbara Andes. Children; Elizabeth, Andrew, Valentine, Joseph, Barbara, Martin, John and Mary.

Michael Biltz and wife Mary Anne Dillor arrived in 1852. Children; Joseph, John, Anna, Mary, Katherine and Eva. From Bomberg Pavaria.

Adam Michael and wife Elizabeth Mink settled here in 1856. Children; Adam, Peter, Margaret, George, Elizabeth, Eva and Lizzie.

Margaret Rose Rietinger came Oct. 2, 1882. Children; Barbara, Magdalene and John. She married Adam Winkler Oct. 12, 1882.

Adam Lansinger came single and married Magdalene Bassel. Children; Mary, Louisa, Anna, Caroline, Martin and William.

Michael Kohl and wife. Children Bartholomew, Katherine, Mary, Eva, Magdelene, Elizabeth, Jacob and Margaret.

Peter Englehart came single and married Elizabeth Lemert. Children; Matilda, Elizabeth, Margaret and Anna.

Valentine Mazel came single and married Katherine Reiz. 6 children Barbara Schweigert, a widow and a child Josephine.

John Bissel and wife Mary Ann Liport. Children 2 girls each named Elizabeth.

Katherine Eck widow. Children; John, Michael and a girl.

Report #3
Father Lindesmith's 1908 financial report

Barkled

DIOCESE OF CLEVELAND

ANNUAL FINANCIAL REPORT.

From *St Peter* Church:

Rootstown Portage co, Ohio.

For the year ending Dec. 31, ~~189~~ *1908*

RECEIPTS.

ORDINARY RECEIPTS.	DOLLARS.	CTS.
To Balance on hand, according to last Financial Report,	270	22
To Cash, Pew Rent,	539	22
" " Sunday Collections,	64	34
" " Papal Collection,	8	93
" " Indian and Negro Missions Collection,	7	02
" " ~~Tuition, or for support of school,~~		
" " Cemetery,	63	00
" " Altar Society dues,	34	61
(Total Ordinary Receipts, $ *987.34*)		

EXTRAORDINARY RECEIPTS.

Collection		
To Cash, ~~Subscriptions~~ for *Slate roof on church*	87	75
" " ~~Extra Collections in the Church,~~		
" " Donations, *Peter Englehart*	102	00
" " ~~Loans, (authorized)~~		
" " ~~Loan, (to cover small discrepancies in closing acc't.)~~		
" " ~~Rents, account church property~~		
" " ~~Interest on church moneys,~~		
" " *Christmas collection*	45	50
" " *Collection for University*	8	17
" " *Paid for a member in 1903: Paid back*	30	00
" " *Rev. E.W.J. Lindesmith donated*	200	06
" "		
" "		
(Total Extraordinary Receipts, $ *476.36*)		
Total Cash Receipts,	$ *1466.76*	

EXPENSES.

ORDINARY EXPENSES.

		DOLLARS.	CTS.
By Cash, Salary of Pastor,		60	00
" " ~~of Teacher,~~			
" " Diocesan Fund,		43	20
" " Infirm Priests' Fund,		5	40
" " Papal Fund, *PAPAL FUND, by the children*		8	93
" " Indian and ~~Negro~~ Missions,		7	92
" " ~~Salary of Sexton,~~			
" " Choir Expenses, *Organist*		20	00
" " Cemetery Expenses, *for labor.*		3	00
" " Mass Wine,		8	00
" " Altar Bread, ~~Candles, Incense and Oil,~~		6	00
" " Altar Ornaments, etc., account Altar Society,		34	00
" " ~~Washing and Repairing Church Vestments,~~			
" " ~~Sweeping and Cleaning Church and School,~~			
" " Light & Fuel for Church, ~~School~~ and Pastoral Res,		28	71
" " Insurance,		35	40
" " Tax,		6	88

(Total Ordinary Expenses, $ 80 746)

EXTRAORDINARY EXPENSES.

		DOLLARS.	CTS.
By Cash, Furniture for Church, ~~School &~~ Pastoral Residence,		22	09
" " Repairs of Church, ~~School~~ and Pastoral Residence,			
" " ~~Building,~~ *Slate roof on church & steeple*		255	89
" " ~~Interest,~~			
" " ~~Amount Paid on debt,~~			
" " *Lumber, Nails, and other furnishings*			
" " *for the roof*		13	25
" " *Collection University at Washington*		8	17
" " *Paid for a church member*		30	00
" "			

(Total Extraordinary Expenses, $ 328 48)

By Total Cash Expended, $ 1136 88

	Pew Rent Due	Pew Rent Paid	Easter Collection	Christmas Collection	Altar Society	Candles and Oil	All Other Collections
Biltz, George	$20 00	$20 00	$1 00	$1 75	$1 20	$1 00	
Biltz, Michael	6 00	6 00	1 00	1 00	1 20	1 00	25
Biltz, John	15 00	15 00	1 00	50			25
Biltz, Dora (S)					1 20		
Biltz, Wm. W. (S)			1 00				
Biltz, G. W. (S)				1 00			
Bower, John	12 00	12 00	1 00	1 00			25
Bower, Adam	14 00	14 00					25
Bower, Barbara Lewis	6 00	6 00		50			
Bassel, Katharine V. (W)	3 00	3 00			1 25		
Bentz, Elizabeth	6 00	6 00	50	1 00	1 20	35	35
Dussel, Mary Peter	12 00	12 00	50	50		50	50
Dussel, John	12 00						
Dussel, Jacob				1 00			
Dussel, Henry W. (S)				1 00			
Engelhart, Peter	4 00	4 00				50	25
Fisher, Mrs John M	6 00	6 00					
Fleshman, Adam	18 00	18 00	1 50	1 50	1 20	1 55	50
Forsch, Julia (S)			1 00				
Friend, A					1 00	20	
Gauer, Charles	6 00	6 00	25	50	1 20	40	10
Gauer, Mrs. Frank	6 00	6 00	50		1 20	25	25
Gauer, John	6 00	6 00					10
Goodier, Barbara	6 00	6 00					
Heisler, William (S)	6 00	6 00		50			
Heisler, Joseph	12 00	12 00	50	60	1 20		25
Hostler, George	6 00	6 00	50			25	25
Hostler, Katharine John					1 75		
Kline, Henry	24 00	24 00	50	1 00	1 25		
Kline, J. B.	12 00	12 00		1 00	1 25		
Kline, George	12 00	12 00	1 00	1 00	1 20	1 00	25
Kline, Henry C.	12 00	12 00	1 00	1 00	1 20	1 00	25
Kline, Charles	12 00	12 00	1 00	2 00	1 25	25	75
Kline, Martin	6 00						25
Knapp, Lawrence	18 00	18 00	1 00	1 30	1 20	50	15
Knapp, Nicholas	18 00	18 00	50	50	1 20		85
Knapp, Adam	6 00	6 00	50	75	1 27		1 00
Knapp, Frank	6 00	6 00					
Knapp, George, Sr.	12 00	12 00	1 00	1 00	1 20	1 50	25
Knapp, George A	12 00	12 00	50	50	1 20	20	
Knapp, Adam E	6 00	6 00	1 00	1 00	1 20	50	25
Knapp, Joseph C	12 00	12 00	50				
Knapp, Frank J	12 00	12 00					
Knapp, Frances (S)					1 20		
Kissel, Barbara (W)	6 00	6 00					
Lansinger, Adam	24 00	24 00	1 00	1 00	1 20	1 00	25
Lansinger, Katharine A (S)					1 20		
Lansinger, Cora Joseph (S)	6 00	6 00	25				
Luli, Henry R	18 00	18 00	50	75	2 45		10
Luli, Joseph (S)	6 00	6 00	50				
Lindesmith, Rev. E. W. J	130 00	130 00					
Miller, Martin, Sr	12 00	12 00		50	1 25	75	10
Miller, Andrew M	12 00	12 00	50	1 00	1 25	40	25
Miller, Martin, Jr.		5 00					25
Miller, Katharine (S)		1 50		50		1 00	25
Miller, Mary (S)		2 00					25
Marquart, Frank	12 00	12 00	1 00	1 00	1 20	70	25
Marquart, Mary (S)	6 00	6 00	50	50	1 20	50	
Marquart, George H	6 00	6 00	50	50			25
May, Edmund	12 00	12 00	50	50			15
Moon, Henry	12 00	12 00					25
Mitch, Aldert	18 00	18 00	50	50	1 20	75	25
Paulus, George	12 00	12 00					
Paulus, Clara (W)	12 00	12 00	50	50			
Palm, Eva (S) Mother (W)	12 00	12 00	50	25	2 40		
Reis, Adam	12 00	12 00	1 00	1 25	1 20		
Reis, Katharine V.(W)	6 00	6 00		1 25	1 20		
Riedinger, John	15 00	15 00	50	1 50	1 20	80	25
Rothemel, Peter	12 00	12 00	1 00	1 75	1 20	1 95	3 85
Rothemel, Frank	6 00	6 00	50				25
Rothemel, Otto	12 00	12 00	25	50	1 25		10
Schrader, Bernard	18 00	18 00	1 00	1 00		75	25
Schmitt, Jacob	24 00	24 00	1 00	2 00	1 20	1 95	50
Winkler, Margaret Adam (W)	6 00	6 00		1 00	1 20		25
Winkler, John	12 00	12 00	1 00	1 00	1 20	25	25
Wiedeman, Bernard	12 00	12 00	1 00	1 00	1 20		25

Louisa Knapp, organist, free of charge. John Wiedeman, 50. M. Edelman, 25. Adam Ecker, 25. Charles Winkler, 25. Ang. Hammer, 50. Frank Treres, 50. John Schefer, 25. Lewis Horning, 25. Lewis Kline, 25. Clement Lang, 25. John F. Lang, 25. George J. Kline, 50. Mrs. Andrew Horning, 30. Mrs. Margaret Long, 25. Mrs. Barbara Kline, 10. J. W. Huth, 25. Frank Paulus, 25. Aloysius Miller, 25. Patrick Fox, 25. John M., 25. M.

Report #4
Interview of Mr. Martin Knipp—
Age 100 when Interviewed

The following interview of Mr. Martin Knipp from Alliance, Ohio, is placed here because of his wife's connection with Father Fowler and the fact that Martin was the oldest known former parishioner when interviewed at age 100 in 2008. It was learned from Martin that Catherine Wohlwend Orgwally from Suffield, Ohio, was Father Fowler's housekeeper. Martin and Catherine were married in 1936 at St. Joseph's, Randolph. Martin, who was born in Austria-Hungry in February 1908, was the son of Adam Knipp and Susan Albitz Knipp. Susan is buried in St. Peter's Cemetery.

Martin came to America in 1910 at age two. The family name had three different spellings: Knipp, Knipf, and Kniph. As mentioned before, some German family names had two or three spellings. Martin had an uncle in the Austro-Hungarian army who was doing guard duty at a particular chalet which Kaiser Wilhelm used as a vacation retreat. When Martin's parents went there to say goodbye to his uncle, it so happened that the Kaiser met them in the lobby and shook Martin's hand. Martin was two years old.

Locating in the St. Peter's area of Rootstown, young Martin worked at dairy and cattle farm, once living very close to the church and once living at the Adam Knapp farm which borders the Winkler farm on what is now called Old Forge Road. He milked cows at the famous Rick's Dairy located just north of Rootstown Center on State Route 44. Martin said the milk was taken by wagon to the train station (most likely Ravenna or New Milford Station) and sent on to New York.

Martin served Mass at St. Peter's for several years starting in 1920. He served with Lawrence Winkler, Clarence Hosler, Paul Heisler, and others. Martin said priests Father Battas (German), Father McGoogan (Irish), and Father Fowler (American) would ask the altar boys to respond in German, Latin, or English when they said the Mass responses.

Martin said he walked to church many times and rang the church bell for the Angeles Prayer which, as stated in an earlier chapter, was done at 6 AM, 12 Noon, and 6 PM on a daily basis for years. Martin Knipp passed away December 26, 2008. His daughter Susan presently lives in Louisville, Ohio.

Report #5
Report from Eloise Sweet Biltz of her recollections of Rootstown

This historical account by Mary Eloise Biltz Sweet regarding her knowledge of Rootstown and its residents is purposely unedited so that the reader can enjoy the writing style and information as she actually presented it.

First, a brief history of my great grandparents— Michael and Mary Ann (Diller) Biils. As related by my father Louis Biltz. They came to Rootstown, Ohio in Portage County in 1852 from Stercken Schweisen, Bomberg, Germany.

My grandfather George Biils was born on the boat outside of New York Harbor. (Imagine the hardships of pregnancy on a boat back then). There were 2-3 or perhaps 4 brothers and their families who came from Bavaria hoping to find a previous group from Alsaice Lorraine who had located at a place called St. Joseph between Randolph and Suffield. They had difficulty finding this place. Somewhere in the vicinity of Warren, Oh. some of them separated, some going west and some south. In not too many days of searching, my great grandfather Michael Biils and a brother Joseph (we think because of a marker in the cemetery at St. Peter's) found the group at St. Josephs. At that time they were unable to trace the others who went westward.

Many years later when Michael's son George was a young man, he went on a trip to Chicago to buy farm equipment. He stopped in South Bend, Indiana, and when he registered at a hotel they questioned him if he was related to Biltz's there. He was interested, knowing the previous history. He stayed over, looked up these Biltz's and discovered that they were the long lost forgotten relatives of his father.

The name was originally BIILS. School teachers argued that you couldn't have 2 i i's together, so it was changed to BILS. Again later teachers asking children their name and in their broken English BILS, became BILTZ.

In the cemetery at St. Peter's there are 3 different spellings of the name and also there are some old legal documents that attest to this.

Michael Biils and his six children settled on a small farm in Rootstown on what is known as Biltz Rd. 2nd road west and to the left off of Tallmadge Rd. and winds around to Old Forge Rd.

He was highly regarded in the community, and served as a township trustee. Disaster struck the family, and their log house burned down. The family then experienced living in the smallest house that ever sheltered a family. This happened about a year after their arrival in Rootstown. Not only the log cabin, but most of its contents burned. They moved into the smoke house— a single room 5 x 7 dimensions, with fur children. They existed here during an entire winter. The rough board table was carried outside for meal time where they stood up to eat. There was no room for chairs. Great grandmother and 3 month old baby slept in the feed house with the cows close by. The rest of the family slept in the hay mow. Unbelievably the family maintained good health.

Michael's sons George, John, and son-in law John Bauer were stone cutters besides farming. With some of their male children they built many bridges over streams in the countryside, plus some of the bridges were built at some distance, it is told that they would be gone for days, and the womenfolk had to carry on with the chores and the like.

Son John Biltz married Elizabeth Michael and lived in Rootstown. His home was next to Mrs. Opfer. They had 3 children all of whom lived in Rootstown. Carl was married to Florence Wertenberger, but died at the birth of a son. There were two sons Richard and Russell. A 2nd marriage was to Grace Loomis, they had two sons Carl Jr. and Claire, daughter Josephine (Josie) married Ray Laird, and lived where Thompsons now live. They also had an apple orchard on New Milford Rd. South and ran a cider press. Robert (Bob) lived next to brother Carl, and later built a stone faced house south of the center.

Daughter Katherine married John Bauer and lived at the corner of Kline Rd. 1st Rd. to the left west on Rte. 18. They had five children Bertha- Mrs. Lou Kline- Brimfield, Abby died in childhood, Ida- Mrs. Joseph Palm who lived a short distance from her parents home on Rte. 18. Wm- (Bill), Florence- Mrs. W. Ross- Akron, Oh.

Other members of Michael's family located in and around St. Josephs, Randolph, and Ravenna:

Eva- Mrs. John Reidinger- lived next to St. Peter's Church. Property acquired from them by the church is where the parish hall and extension of cemetery.

George Bils- 3rd son of Michael (my grandfather) remained in Rootstown- married Elizabeth Basel and lived across the road from his father Michael. Some of his 6 children remained in Rootstown to make their home here.

Oldest son Henry lived at the corner of Biltz Rd. and old 18. Henry married Gertrude White and had five children, Albert- Kent, Oh. Herbert- Brimfield, Oh. Frank- Atwater, Oh. Mildred- Mrs. Stanley Whittlesey- Monroe, Oh. Florence- Mrs. Frank Stenger- Yorba Linda, Calif.

Second daughter of George- Dora- married Joseph Luli, and resided on several farms in Rootstown. Last one on the corner of Old Forge and Hartville Rd. Now the Teeters home. Children were Beatrice- Mrs. Sylvan Kline- Rootstown, Mrs. Clara (Charles) Miller-Suffield, Lucille- Mrs. Herbert Kline- Canton, Oh. Robert- Ravenna, Oh. Hilda- Mrs. Roy Taylor- Ashtabula, Oh.

Another son Louis (my father) married Matilda Weideman and ran a garage in Rootstown for over 60 years. Children were Mary Eloise R.N.- Mrs. Floyd Sweet- Rootstown. Thelma E. worked for Monsignor Delmege for 45 yrs- now lives in Naples, Fl.

George's daughter Clara- single died at the age of 18 on the operating table for appendicitis. George's son Rudolph married Clara Knapp, and resided on the homestead, and had eight children, some of whom still live in Rootstown. Alma- Mrs. Lawrence Winkler- Canton, Oh. Winifred- Mrs. Robert Kaltenbach- Rootstown (her husband was Fire Chief for 30 yrs.) Mary Catherine- Mrs. Maurice Knapp- Denver, Co. Charles- Rootstown (sons Jerry and Michael, and Kathy live in Rootstown). Richard- passed away in manhood, Isobel- Mrs. Guy Moore- Rootstown (son David, and Judy- Mrs. David Common live in Rootstown) Betty- Mrs. Gerald King (daughters Janet- Mrs. Berta- lives on her great grandfather's place, and Janet- Mrs. Popschiel- lives in Rootstown) Shirley- Mrs. Elmer Riemenschneider (Elmer is township supervisor of roads and sexton of cemetery).

There are a few interesting tales related by my dad from his repertory of memories. Dad and his brothers and sisters were on their way home from attending catechism classes at St. Peter's. They were skating on ice in the ditches along the roadway. Some boys had made holes in the ice, and my dad fell through. Soaking wet, his brothers and sisters ran him home, which was a considerable piece. He was a frozen ice-sculpture when they got him home. He was packed in blankets, hot stones, and straw, and fortunately survived. My grandfather sought out the culprit and threatened the law if Dad didn't make it.

Another story was when my grandmother, a short, heavy-set woman was milking and the cow kicked over her bucket of milk. In her anger, she swatted the cow, who took off with grandmother holding onto her tail. She was dragged down the orchard lane until rescued by her children—easily could have been killed, but fortunately not and lived to be 90 yrs. old.

Dad related that he cut his foot badly and was bleeding excessively. Grandmother went to the chicken coop, gathered up some cobwebs, and put them on the wound—bleeding was controlled.

Someone developed blood poisoning, red streaks up the person's arm. Navy beans were cooked up and a poultice placed on the infected area overnight. The beans turned black and the person recovered.

Rendered lard was also used to heal many times. I grew up with the use of lard for medicinal purposes.

Back to other recollections of my life in Rootstown.

I was 2-3 yrs. old when my father, Lewis Biltz bought the Babb property lot 21 in Rootstown. I can recall moving to Rootstown from Kent, Oh. My Uncle Ed May ran a moving and storage business so naturally he moved us in a big moving van. I got to sit in that big van, and oh you could see so much more.

My Dad and my uncle Clarence Weideman were engaged in running a garage south of Rootstown center for several years. It was located in the basement of the once school house, where the town hall now stands. (I can vaguely remember a few years later when it burned down.)

In 1922-1923, my folks bought the Babb property, Dad bought out my uncle and established his own business. He, with the help of many relatives, moved the barn nearer to the highway (Route 44) and opened his garage, which he maintained for 60 years plus.

I can remember having to go out and crawl under an automobile to hold a light for Dad to see, and I was not really a Tomboy. I marvel at this man who crawled under cars with his creeper to repair cars in all kinds of weather. I recall when he installed a furnace in the garage and one could stand close to it to warm up. Believe me there was no insulation in the garage. Also recall having to help pump gasoline by hand 5-10 gals. into the automobile. Once in a while someone would give you a nickel or dime tip— candy money.

Dad lived to be 97 plus and no arthritis or rheumatism. He insisted on eating pork and sauerkraut once a week. And in the spring lots of dandelions which mother would wilt with lard.

In later years when auto's didn't have broken bearings, transmissions or rear ends that gave out he added to his skills blacksmithing. I remember that anvil where sparks would fly and one would have to stand back so as not to get burned by the sparks. We girls had to turn the blower. He created many of his own tools which he hammered out. He also acquired and self taught the skill of welding with an acetylene torch. He would heat up a piece of steel, and then plunge it into oil or water to temper it. At one time he got the idea to put steel points on plow shears to make them last longer. (The steel points came from old automobile springs.) Soon he had requests from all around Portage County. Sometimes he would run short on oxygen and would go to Louisville or Canton and get a tank of oxygen.

I can recall the trips to Akron to an auto supply house for parts. My sister and I took turns going along for that ride. On the way home Dad would stop at an Acme store for peanuts in the shell and sometimes chunks of milk chocolate, which was half eaten by the time we arrived home to share with mother and sister.

I can remember when Rte 18, now Tallmadge Rd (running east and west thru Rootstown) was constructed. Dad had the contract to supply gasoline for the trucks and shovels. I recall a spanking I got for this, because in my enchantment I failed to answer my mother's call.

Then the accidents started. Many of them at the crossroads. One in particular I recall when some big wheel from Youngstown came speeding thru the center, hit someone and continued traveling between our house and Mrs. Winick's and hit a huge willow tree in the back yard.

Dad had a wrecker that he made from a Hupmobile car. He was called out to   pick up wrecked cars and cars in ditches at all hours of the day and night. Also many nights there were frantic knocks at the door—someone had run out of gas and Dad would dress and go out and give them gas, sometimes take gas to a car left on the side of the road.

We went to St. Peter's Catholic Church which is located on Old Forge Rd. off of Hartville Rd. (second rd to the right south of Rootstown which was established in 1868.) I am told that as a 2 ½ yr old I asked "where were we going?" and was told to "St. Peter's". On Sunday when we went to Mass and I saw Father Battes walking from the rectory to the church I popped off "Look there is St. Peter" and for years I was teased about this.

Mother and Dad were very active and faithful members of St. Peter's. Dad was a councilman for 40 years. Mother and Thelma sang in the choir. Mother was president of the Alter and Rosary Society for many years. Mother also took care of the alter linens and flowers for so many years. No weather was too bad to get to church. On Saturday mornings we were taken to church for Catechism. Mother and Father drilled us daily in learning our prayers and the questions and answers in the Baltimore Catechism. Father Battes of German descent was a strict teacher— you better have it memorized before you got there.

Then we would walk back to my Uncle Joe Luli's farm to wait for Dad when he was free to come and get us. We used to pick violets, forget me nots, and pussy willows along the roadside to bring to my grandmother who lived with aunt Dora. And my aunt always had a large pie crust cookie for us. Wish I could make them.

Father Battes was moved to Canal Fulton and Father Siegfred Heyl came. I made my 1st Holy Communion when Father Heyl was pastor. Father Walter Fowler followed Father Heyl. At that time St. Peter's was a very small parish, thru his efforts of bringing back parishioners who had strayed to Ravenna and St. Joseph the parish grew. The hard work of the women of the parish should also be noted. They served chicken dinners 3-4 times a summer. Crowds of 300 up to 600 were served. It was tremendous hard work on kerosene stoves. They called some of them "socials". I can remember that at one of these socials I had my taste of an Eskimo Pie.

We also had a group that put on 3 act plays for several years under Father Fowler. One was "Abby's Irish Rose" and I was Abby. Mother and Dad also acted in these plays. Another was a mystery play and I was hanging in a closet by my hair. When someone opened the closet door I let out a blood curdling scream.

Father Fowler was asked by the School to give the Commencement address one year. He gave a remarkable address, and it was remembered by townsfolk in Rootstown for many years. He obtained the Reidinger property next door and enlarged the cemetery. The men of the parish planted daffodils all around the cemetery. A beautiful sight in the spring. Father Fowler passed away in 1941, and is buried at his choice—St. Peter's addition to the cemetery, in front of an Altar constructed in the cemetery, with a beautiful backdrop of trees and shrubbery.

He was succeeded by Father Robert Delmege, who did a lot of renovation of the parish buildings. The vestibule of the front of the church was enlarged, and extended over the steps leading into the church. Improvements in the sacristy, and the front porch of the rectory enclosed and made into an office. My sister Thelma had assisted Father Fowler as a housekeeper and aid to Father Fowler's mother who lived with him. Father Delmege asked her to stay on for a couple of weeks. Instead, she stayed on as his housekeeper for 45 years. Father Delmege was moved to Louisville, Oh.

Father Pat Gallagher, Father Thomas McNally, Father Gerald Cawley served as administrators. Father Tomash followed Father Delmege. Father Allen Simpson came in 1964. He was a negro priest who had been in Kent, Oh. He was highly thought of in the community. He had a sudden death at a convention in Chicago. The parish hall was built when Father Cawley was here. He was succeeded by Father Michael Gawron, and then by Father John Sargent. Much of the work that has been done at St. Peter's has remarkably been done by parishioners.

Back to the center of Rootstown. Grandmother Mary Winick had the small house around the corner from us. Her well was just outside of our kitchen window. She was well up in years and not in good health. She had two sons from a former marriage. Harry in Akron, and Jack living in the state of Washington. Mr. and Mrs. Jack Purrington with their two children Mary and Dick came to take care of Grandma Winick. Jack and his wife built a successful restaurant, and called it the Maple Tree Lodge, on the corner of Rte 44 and 18. It was built by Carl and Bob Biltz. I well remember my first job. Working for Purington's—washing dishes, later graduated into waiting on tables. I was even trusted with son Dick for a few hours sometimes while Mr. and Mrs. Purington went to a movie. On the other side of the Winick house another garage (in the 40's) was built and run by Ding Sabin. On the corner of routes 44 and 18, a filling station sprung up run by Mr. Anderson, who lived south of the center.

I recall the Dr. Power's property on the other side of the Methodist Church. A Mr. and Mrs. Avery also run a small store in a building out front. Mr. and Mrs. Grady Allen and daughter Gladys moved there later. They run the store and the post office was located at one end operated by Mr. Peck. Later the post office was moved into the Winick house after grandma Winick passed away. Gertrude Deming was post mistress there and Mr. Allen got and delivered the mail when it was deposited off the train at New Milford. Mr. Allen ran a barbershop in his home, and later built a barbershop and the post office where the K of C hall now stands. They also built a home south of the center.

Rootstown was the home of the Reich Dairy. They had three farms. One north of the center on the land where Baronwood Plaza now stands. Mr. G. Moser also had a dairy there. One south of the center next to Bower Rd. This had a huge house and barns on 44 and on Bower Rd. where Wittaker and Turk live. Some of their production was certified milk that was sent to Pittsburgh. The other barn and large house was southeast on Diagonal Rd. now Cook Rd. It was at the top of the hill. Later Ellsworth lived there and still later Harville's. I can well remember the night that the big barn on 44 was struck by lightning. It was quite an awesome night.

The large general store and gas station across the street from us was 1st run by my recollection by Henry Michael family and they lived in what is now known as the Forte house. Later they moved about a half mile south of the center where Friedl's now live. The store was later run by a Mr. and Mrs. Harrison. Followed by Mr. and Mrs. Long and a Mr. Pratt. Troxel family lived in the house when the Longs lived in the Seymour house where Kaltenbacks now live. Mr. and Mrs. Don Filmore and Mrs. Miller lastly run the store. Attached to the store was a restaurant run by Ma Sterling who served 3.2 beer.

Where the Fire Station now stands was a small coffee and sandwich shop run by Mrs. Llewelyn. Someone sold firecrackers on the outside before the Fourth. One night the firecrackers caught fire and burned the restaurant down. That was quite an explosion of sky rockets etc.

I can't recall all of the ministers at the Methodist Church next door, with their rectory across the street. I do remember that there were a lot of oak trees next to the Church where they parked cars for services. Reverend Williams and his family lived there with his son and wife and two children. The son was called "Hawkshaw" because of his interest in detective work. He was followed by Reverend Springer and family, they were very friendly and their son used to come over to watch television. I believe after them the house was sold to Joe Kerr and family, and the minister moved west of the center.

I do vaguely remember the ice cream room that Yarian's ran, but I do recall a lot of hours spent there playing with Mary Louise May Shaw. Later it was turned into a one room apartment and a widowed Mr. Mitchell lived there. He committed suicide there. He had a daughter Ruth, a classmate of mine who went blind.

Mrs. Opfer owned the big white house next to the Fire Station. Her adopted son Brian Jones was a young man living with her. Next to her was Uncle John and Elizabeth Biltz's home later owned by Mr. and Mrs. Sheffield—next was the Seymour home, later Mr. and Mrs. Long and then Bob and Winnie Kaltenback.

Mr. and Mrs. Wallace Ott lived across the street—the back end of our property joined the side of theirs. Mrs. Ott used to watch for the light in our kitchen window.

I can recall when we moved into our house. It had one electric light in the ceiling of each room downstairs and one light on a sidewall in the two rooms upstairs. This house which I still live in is a historical place. Back in the 1850-60's it was a tavern, and upstairs a Dr. Bassett had an office. We had a cistern pump in the kitchen and a large wood and coal stove with an attached water reservoir to heat water. Well remember coming down from upstairs bedrooms to dress and bathe in front of the oven door.

We used hot bricks or irons wrapped in paper to put in bed during the cold nights. Dad added a hot water tank heated by coal particularly for laundry purposes. We had a hot air furnace using coal. We had a large register in the living room and a smaller one in the dining room. There was a register above the one in the living room to allow some warm air to get to the upstairs. Later we had a stoker for coal and still later Dad installed a hot water system for heating. When gas was available our stoker was exchanged for a gas furnace.

Dad put in an electric water pump and added baseboard receptacles for electricity. Installed a bathroom upstairs with a septic tank out behind the chicken house.

For a few years we had pigs and butchered them for our meat. I remember the crocks of sausage and liverwurst. Butchering was quite an affair with my uncles and aunts coming to help. Mother also used to can beef when we could get a quarter of beef from my uncle when he butchered a cow. Also had chickens, our own eggs and meat. I recall with distaste having to dunk a dead chicken in a bucket of hot water and remove the feathers. Also couldn't stand to see a chicken killed by chopping off its head, and I never could do that. But we truly enjoyed Mothers Sunday chicken dinner. It was always special to get baby chicks at Cotton Corners and watch them grow.

I have been told by Amanda Jennings who once lived in this house, that during the Civil War it was a tavern and that a Dr. Basset had offices on the second floor.

The Horton homes east of the center had a secret room to hide slaves coming thru from the south. Margaret Horton and I were and still are special friends and I spent many happy hours at that place. I remember the two seater swing on the side yard. We used to walk to school together and come home and spend hours talking. About what I don't recall. When we got to high school and were permitted to have parties, Margaret and I would usually have one party for classmates every other year. Mrs. Horton would make ice cream for that party, and many a time I helped to churn delicious ice cream. Also in the fall we had weiner roasts. I remember some at Lucille Ely and Genevieve Grant's homes.

How good our parents were. We of course had no cars, but they would take us and later come to pick us up from these class parties.

Mr. and Mrs. Shrigley and children lived next door to Horton's. My sister and Eileen were classmates. I recall one time being there and I saw Jello made for the first time. Later their oldest son was tragically killed in a takeoff crash at Akron airport.

I remember "Pinky" (don't know why he had that name) Seymour who lived north of the center on what was the Polumbo property and now where McDonalds is. He was a little queer, but very bright and he would ride his horse around town.

I remember Chan Seymour and his farm west of the center. He had a small furniture business in their home. My folks bought several pieces of furniture from them. I recall being there and seeing a small bronze desk lamp that was movable. Thought it was the greatest thing and begged my parents to get it for me for Christmas. I still have that lamp and use it. My Dad used to tell a story about Chan Seymour. He called Dad at 3 am to come out and start his riggity truck. He was taking a load of pigs to market in Cleveland. After Dad got the truck to run, he asked for help in loading the pigs. Dad couldn't envision how? No problem he took a pitch fork and run it down a pigs back and he run right up an inclined plank into the truck.

Also remember Reverend Robinson from the Congregational Church. Highly respected by members he later retired and chose Rootstown as his home in retirement.

Next to the Congregational ministers home was the Spelman house where Asa Spelman and daughter Mary lived. They were prominent people in Rootstown. Mary a lovely single lady adopted Angelo— a little Italian boy. Angelo used to come into the garage when Dad ran one south of the center. Dad taught him to count in German, and Angelo taught Dad to count in Italian. Angelo would always stop in to see my Dad and chat and even in my Dad's later years, they would always count.

Not to forget Hazel Gerren-Dutch Gerrens wife who lived next to Josie Laird. She was a very special lady. She worked for Purrington's in the restaurant. She worked in the school cafeteria. She was widowed and raised 4 children. Bob, Pauline, Lucille, and James- who still lives in Rootstown on Marks Ave. Thelma and I used to play with Pauline and Lucille.

Out at the top of the hill west of the center was Mrs. Dickerson who had a very crippled daughter Maria. I recall seeing this woman struggling to get to the post office.

Also remember the Dundon's east of the center. This was Margaret Horton's aunt and uncle. Mr. Dundon would come over to the garage and discuss the world's events with my Dad. Next to them was Jack McManus and family— Mrs. McManus and daughter Leah Somers live in Rootstown today. Mr. McManus had a small machine shop in the back of his home.

The Finch home was also east of the center, and Miss Bertha Bradshaw— 1st grade teacher lived with her sister Mrs. Finch, north of the center where the Guither family lived. A daughter Areleen Semon married a Finch. The Finches had a cabin at Lake Milton and classes at school went there for a final school year.

I spent 11 years in Rootstown School with oh so many memories which I share with classmates at our reunions. The wonderful teachers we had. Yes I was one of the thousands that Bertha Bradshaw started out in first grade. Miss Newell, Mrs. Tarr, Gertrude Deming—a

Rootstown woman who spent many years teaching, and later as a post mistress in Rootstown. She lived to be close to the goal of 100. Miss Ungar— 6th grade teacher was here for many years— appreciated by having one of the school buildings named after her. Mr. Van Deusen— he gave me a powder box for perfect attendance. Ward Davis— principal— married local girl Helen Parsons. Highly regarded. Became a lawyer. Mrs. Cox— Home Economics teacher, Miss Hall, Mrs. Hanna Ot— married a Rootstown man, and both continued teaching in other communities. Mr. Perkins was a class advisor. But especially Mr. Heritage was special, he was a class advisor, science teacher, and for many years he was principal. He married a Rootstown gal Isobel Ward. He attended our class reunions and we always welcomed his wonderful personality.

We had the privilege of coming home for lunch, because we lived close to the school, but it was a real treat on rare occasions to take your lunch to school. I also vaguely remember being at my Uncle Rudy's farm and riding to school in the school hack driven by horses.

Mrs. Cox organized some women in the community to give of their time once a week to make school lunches. My mother volunteered. In the Home Ec's class in the fall we would can vegetables for use in the cafeteria.

How many of those people plus my wonderful parents who guided us through those formative years we owed a debt of gratitude as we recall memories, and memories, and memories of Rootstown.

This brings me up to my senior year. I was given the privilege of attending a private boarding school—Villa Maria High School in Pennsylvania. I went to Cleveland to attend nursing school at St. Alexis, and in three years I graduated an R.N.

Even though most of my years 41 in all in nursing in Cleveland, I lived at home in Rootstown, I was away from home 10-12 hours a day riding the Dan Hanna commuter train that stopped in New Milford Station, later I took the train from Ravenna and when the Pennsylvania train discontinued we drove to Mantua to take the Erie into Cleveland. In 1966 I started to drive back and forth to Cleveland to work until my retirement in 1982.

Lots of years, though I lived in Rootstown, and knew everyone and where they lived, I now realize that the town has grown up and away from me to the point that I find I don't know who some neighbors are.

The community now has Settlers Days— and yes it is wonderful to see faces and try to put names to them. To see old antiques, that bring back memories. No we are not old, but we have recollected many, many memories of Rootstown.

Report #6
Soldiers serving from St. Peter's in WWII by Father Delmege

July
1943

Dear Parishioner:

     1) May the blessings of God visit the homes of those who are interested in their Parish enough to make splendid sacrifices to support it! To each and every one who is, I, your Pastor, extend my deepest gratitude! It is my hope that those who are "sponging" on the generosity of such people will soon begin to take up their share of the running expenses of our Church.

     2) Do not forget that our weekly evening Devotions in Honor of the Sacred Heart and the Divine Infancy of Jesus (Miraculous Infant of Prague) is for an early Peace and the Safe Return of ALL of our boys in the armed forces. In your private prayers, too, beg the Sacred Heart to protect them and bring all of them safely back to their homes. We now have sixteen:

Angebrandt,	John
Bello,	Charles
Bildershein,	Charles
Bildershein,	George
Bildershein,	Michael
Caprez,	John
Esposito,	Albert
Esposito,	Louis
Kline,	Harold
Knapp,	Paul
Knapp,	Roy
Leyland,	Jack
Moledor,	John
Moledor,	Paul
Polack,	Andrew
Polack,	Joseph

     3) Many seem to have forgotten that lacking a regular janitor it is necessary for the men to assist in working about the Parish buildings and the church yard!

     4) Thanks be to the good God, all things considered, you have done a grand job these past two years!

Report #7
St. Peter's Youth Group, barn dances by Joan & Marie Rice
ST. PETER'S YOUTH CLUB, THE OLD BARN, ROCK 'N' ROLL, CHRISTMAS PLAYS AND BINGO

Memories of Marie Rice and Joan Rice, twin daughters of a long-time St. Peter of the Fields parishioner, the late Nancy Rice

A '57 Chevy speeds around the rolling curves of Old Forge Road. It's a warm summer night in 1960. Eddie Cochran's "Summertime Blues" blares from the radio tuned to WHK Cleveland. But Cochran is no match for the rock 'n' roll sounds emanating from St. Peter's old barn. The novelty hit "The Purple People Eater" drowns out the car's small radio speaker. The song tells the story of a "one-eyed, one-horned, flying, purple, people eater" who descends to earth yearning to join a rock 'n' roll band. Travelers along Old Forge Road by now know St. Peter's Youth Club is holding another rock 'n' roll barn dance.

The teens from St. Peter's C.Y.O. (Catholic Youth Organization) like teenagers everywhere are also watching Dick Clark's "American Bandstand" and perfecting all the latest dance crazes. Copying local high schools, St. Peter's young people defied propriety and staged their very own "Rock 'n' Roll Record Hops" in the old bard on the recently acquired property next to St. Peter of the Fields Church. The old pine plank floor, where farmers once stacked bales of hay, plays host now to teenagers from the surrounding community dancing "The Fast Dance," "The Stroll" and "The Calypso." On one summer night in 1960, St. Peter's teenagers strung yards of multi-colored crepe paper from beam to wooden beam, creating a Hawaiian theme. The club's public relations machine went to work, posting the details of the big dance in the window of Fillmore's General Store at the Rootstown Center, a favorite teen hangout. Admission charge? 50 cents.

There was only enough money in the small Youth Club treasury to purchase a few 45 RPM records, so St. Peter's teenagers volunteered to bring music from their own personal record collections. One could hear all the Billboard hits of the day blasting through the cracks and open door of the old barn: Bobby Darin's "Splish Splash," "Fats Domino's "Blueberry Hill," Chunky berry's "Sweet Little Sixteen," The Fleetwoods' "Come Softly to Me," the Kalen Twins' "When." Sounds of the Coasters, Ricky Nelson, Duane Eddy, Jerry Lee Lewis, Fabian, Jan and Dean, the Everly brothers, Buddy Holly and, of course, the King of Rock 'n' Roll, Elvis Presley also set feet flying on the old wooden floor. One night the exuberant crowd, swept up by the dynamism of the music, spontaneously formed a conga line and gleefully danced out the door into the parking lot. They didn't return until they had circled the old barn a couple of times. Youth Club member Charles Miley spun all the rock 'n' roll discs on his own portable record player. St. Peter's youth were there for the birth of rock 'n' roll and its musical revolution…and they were proud of it.

In the late 1950s, the youth club held a few dances in the basement of the church. And after youth club meetings on Thursday nights, teens often spun a few records and danced. Among youth club members at the time were Charles Miley, Helen Winkler, Rose Winkler, Ronnie Knapp, Paul Moskal, Bill Kline, Ray Luli, Marie Rice and Joan Rice. The gang planned many social events, including a memorable hayride through the area's scenic country roads.

The old church hall was also the scene of weekly bingo. The youth club donated its time and talent to serve refreshments. The menu was simple: popcorn, chips, pretzels and pop. Youth club members took turns working the bingo shift, popping huge pots of popcorn, adding butter, then quickly filling dozens of small brown paper bags. In those days, the root beer and Nehi orange, grape and cherry soda came in tall glass bottles. Sometimes balancing trays of the hot bagged popcorn and unwieldy bottles proved to be a challenge. Occasionally bingo players would try to tip the servers (not the victims, of course, of accidentally spilled sticky, orange soda) but we assured them "all the pop they could drink" was payment enough.

One Christmas, on the small stage in the church basement, the youth club performed a yuletide play for St. Peter's parishioners. The highlight came when the play's lines called for cutting and serving up a slice of plum pudding, just like the one made famous by Mrs. Cratchit in Dickens' timeless "A Christmas Carol." Not having a clue where to find plum pudding, inventive youth club members decided to substitute black cherry Jell-O (not a good idea.) When 11-year-old John Rice struggled to cut the slippery substitute, snickers started in the back of the hall. Intense and serious, undeterred by the titters and refusing to give up, John labored on— unfortunately, unsuccessfully. The chortles now gained momentum. Soon the entire audience was engulfed in uproarious laughter. Now thinking he was ruining the scene, John just gave up and plopped the entire hunk of Jell-O on the plate as one BIG slice. The curtain came down as the laughter continued. Backstage, John was mortified, not realizing he had become the star of the show. We'll always cherish these treasured memories of more innocent times.

Report #8
Holy Land and Crucifix painting on the wall at the front of the historic church by Mary Kline Roynesdal
4/24/1997

In the spring of 1978 Father Michael Gawron commissioned me to paint the oil painting behind the cross at St. Peter of the Fields Church. He wanted a reproduction of the painting which was there between the years of 1950 to 1968. We think that Father Delmege had it painted, but in 1968 Father Allen Simpson had the church repainted and the painting was covered over.

Father Gawron had slides and photographs of the original painting. After looking at the slides, I agreed that the painting could be reproduced. So, that summer, after completing my junior year in college, I returned to Rootstown to begin the commission.

Our plan was to use a slide projector to show the slide onto the wall behind the cross, then draw the picture right onto the wall from the slide. After which, I would have painted the painting directly onto the wall. (That would have been too easy.) However, our plan didn't work. The slide was not sharp enough to be projected that large. It just looked like a big blur. So-o-o, back to square one.

Father Gawron had the slide made into an 8x10 photograph. He also decided, in the meantime, that I should do the painting on masonite, so that it could be removed and saved if another priest (in the future) decided to have it painted over again!

In June of that year I began work on the painting. In the basement of the church, I leaned the masonite up against the wall and worked free hand from the photograph. The painting was done in oils. Father Gawron would stop in every day to see how the painting was coming along. He specifically wanted cherub-like angels in the clouds. These were not in the original painting, but Father had seen them in an original "Raphael" painting in the Vatican Museum in Rome. He wanted these angels in his painting. So, I did my best. Each day he would come in with some kind of joke about when I could complete the work. I would laugh and say, "When I'm Finished!" (Like Michelangelo answered the Pope when he did the Vatican.)

Finally in mid-July of 1978 the painting was completed and hung. (John Luli actually did the hanging for us). Father Gawron was extremely happy with the completed work. And I was glad to be finished! (I was paid $500.00 for the completed work.)

Later that year I added the clouds on either side of the painting near the ceiling. This was to help the painting blend in better. The clouds were done in oils directly on the wall.

The gold border around the painting was added a year later by Mary, Rose, and Betty King, to add the finishing touches.

Report #9
The Passion Play by Helen White (2005)

Father Thomas Crum initiated the first theatrical production of *The Passion of Our Lord According to St. John* in 2005. Father Tom wrote the script for the play, with thanks to St. John the Gospel writer and produced and directed the play as "A Crum Production." He entitled the group of young people, St. Peter of the Field Youth Theater Guild. Rehearsals were serious as Father Tom imparted religious insight and feeling into the young actors. The productions took place in the social hall on Friday, March 18, and Saturday, March 19, 2005.

The following year, Father Tom was transferred to Our Lady of Peace in Canton. Despite the lack of his leadership, the young people wanted to do the production again. They worked very hard to put on a very prayerful performance.

The third year, the same enthusiasm arose amongst the young people and once again they showed up for rehearsal on time and seriously endeavored to capture the story of Jesus' final days, Crucifixion and Resurrection. This year we added the scene at the tomb where the angels appear and then Mary Magdalene encounters Jesus. As the play ended, the crowd of young actors, who had followed Jesus, emerged from back stage and went to tell the audience that "HE HAS RISEN." Kalli Dreger, in particular, stopped at each person in every row, put her hands on their shoulders, and with passion and sincerity, spread the news. It was very moving. And give credit to all, the narrator, the sound production person, each wonderful actor and set designer and participant including the mothers behind the scene. It was truly a meaningful experience.

Certainly the youth of the parish will continue to make this play part of their Lenten experience for years to come.

Report #10
A Dream Come True by Robert F. Winkler, book author
The story of the new shrine in St. Peter's cemetery.
Note: See Photo Section, Photos #29 and #30

Replacing the cross and building the structure over the altar at the cemetery of St. Peter of the Fields Catholic Church, Rootstown, Ohio.

When Father John Sargent was our priest, several discussions took place concerning the needed repair to the large cemetery cross. John Duffy, Elmer Riemenschneider, Roy Paulus, Vernon Clapp, and Chuck Miley were some of our parishioners involved in these discussions.

The cross and altar were originally constructed in 1941, when Father Robert Delmege was our pastor. The photo in the church archives shows Father Delmege and Louis Biltz working on the altar with cement trowels in hand.

In December of 1999, Bob Winkler Sr. initiated a conversation with Henry Kline about the need to replace the cross. Henry and Bob then cut down a large locust tree on the Kline farm. Bob hauled the log to Custom Lumber in Atwater where Mr. Chad Roberts, Mill Operator, cut the log into an 18 foot, 8" x 10" piece and an 8 foot, 8" x 10" piece for the new cross. This was done at no cost to the church.

The two log pieces were then hauled to Bob Winkler Jr.'s farm on Old Forge Road for storage so the wood could dry out. Two years later the pieces were transported to Jim Winkler's garage in Brimfield, where Jim notched, sanded, and fashioned the two pieces into a new cross. Jim also stained the wood with preservative and tamarack coloring.

On November 5, 2000, Jeff Knapp and Barney Trares took down the old cross and crucifix. Jeff furnished his truck, trailer, and backhoe for this tedious job. The crucifix was in need of repainting and was, therefore, transported to Strip Master Blasting Company in Randolph by Bob and Jim Winkler. Owner/Operator Jerry Schlarb sand blasted the crucifix in his shop at no cost to the church.

Lee Jenior from Jenior Ford then transported the crucifix to his paint and body shop where it was painted metallic gold at no cost. The crucifix was then temporarily stored in the church basement boiler room. The date was November 24, 2000. On November 29, 2000, Steve Francis dug the 5 foot hole for the cross. He furnished his truck, trailer, and hole digger at no cost.

A serious problem then developed with the County Building Department; work was put on hold. Finally, on August 22, 2001, Bob and Jim Winkler placed the new cross and painted crucifix into position with the assistance of Bill Conroy. Bob Winkler furnished the Winkler farm backhoe and several ropes.

Several months earlier, on November 9, 2000, Bob Winkler Sr. met with Larry Mudd, parishioner and a cement contractor, and took measurements for a cement extension to the back side of the altar. This was to provide space for the priest to stand behind the altar for mass and other services. During this time period, Father Sargent had retired and Father Tom Crum had been installed as Pastor. Father Crum had requested the extra altar extension. Mr. Mudd provided the concrete and the labor for this at no cost.

After several trips were made by Bob and Jim Winkler to the Portage County Building Department and along with other meetings that included Janet Esposito, Chris Smeiles, and

Kathleen Chandler, all county officials; a variance hearing was finally scheduled in Akron, Ohio, October 25, 2001. The proposed structure was finally approved at this meeting, which was attended by Jim Winkler. Building permits and plans cost $485.

Four holes that were three feet deep were dug by Jim Winkler, Bill Conroy, and Jim Nestich. Four 8" x 8", four foot steel sleeves were then cemented into place to support the structure's four 8" x 8" wooden posts. Concrete was delivered by Horning's Supply in Ravenna. The wooden posts and the roof boards were purchases from Gale House Lumber in Doylestown. The wooden beams and other lumber were delivered by True Value Lumber in Hartville. The roof shingles were purchased from O'Conner's Roofing in Mogadore. The wood was treated and stained by Jim Winkler.

During the months of November and December of 2001, Bob and Jim Winkler, Barney Trares, Jim Nestich, and Bill Conroy erected the new structure over the altar. A man, who wishes to remain unnamed, shingled the roof. The entire structure is a brown rustic color.

A ditch, 660 feet in length, was dug from the hall to the shrine. An electric line and 100 amp service was installed. Michael Justice, assisted by two of his own employees, did this work. There was no cost to the church.

A water line was also installed at this same time. The line was purchased by Vernon Clapp at Porter Metal. Vernon furnished his tractor to close the ditch. The cost to the church for the water line was $250.

Earlier in the summer, several trees, about 30, were removed along the west side of the cemetery to make room for 40 more gravesites. This work was accomplished by Steve Francis with his large track hoe and skid loader. Also assisting was Jim and Bob Winkler, Bill Conroy, and one of Steve's employees. About the same time, Bob, Jim, and Bill cut down and removed approximately 25 large pines immediately northwest of the cemetery for additional future grave space. Both work areas were then prepared and seeded by Bob, Jim and Bill.

Total cost of the shrine to the church was $4785; total donations to the project by the workers were in excess of $5000.

Mass was first celebrated by Father Tom Crum on Memorial Day 2002. See Ch. XI (Photo Section, Photos #29 and #30) for photos of the construction of this altar and shrine.

Those Who Truly Believe

As the crucifix was being prepared for painting, it was positioned on the floor of the body shop at Jenior Ford Randolph and covered with a tarp. Owner Lee Jenior said that during this time, there was no loud talking or swearing inside the shop. One day Lee told his brother Mitch to come with him to the body shop and help him move the crucifix off the floor to a more secure and respectable location. Lee had arranged for one of his shop employees who had shoulder length hair to lie down on the floor and cover up with the tarp. Needless to say, the crucifix had already been moved to a secure place.

Upon entering the shop, Lee told Mitch to take one arm of the crucifix and he would take the other and they would move it to another location. As Mitch began to lift the arm, the Jenior employee sat straight up. Lee said Mitch's eyes got about as big as saucers.

A few days later, Bob hauled the painted crucifix back to the church basement. Because the arms were too wide to slide the entire crucifix inside his truck, they were positioned across the tailgate with a pad underneath the head to keep it from bouncing around. As Bob drove north on SR44 at about 40 mph, a fast approaching motorist came up behind and suddenly backed off and held that position until Bob turned left on Bassett Road. Bob said the driver looked intently at the back of the truck as he reduced his speed.

Bob then drove across Bassett Road at a very slow speed, as the road was very bumpy. Another motorist came up behind and followed at 15-20 mph until Bob turned north on Hartville Road. His eyes were also intently fixed on the back of Bob's truck.

Summary of Costs
$485-Permits and Architecture drawings
$400-Concrete for four footers and posts
$225-Steel sleeves for support posts
$1500-Support Posts and Roof boards
$1500-4" x 10" timbers for framework
$425-Roof shingles
$250-Water line
Total-$4785
$5000+ was donated in materials and labor

Report #11
Heritage Preservation Committee report by Helen White

In the fall of 2005 at the September 14th meeting of the Parish Council, a discussion was held concerning the importance of preserving the parish's heritage. An ad hoc committee, the Heritage Preservation Committee, was to be commissioned by the Parish Council and charged with these duties:
   -To research and document the history of the parish
   -To research funding opportunities related to the Historical Register
   -To recommend a plan for creating an endowment that would provide   the care and upkeep of the Historic Church.

At the following meeting October 11, 2005, it was announced that the ad hoc committee for the endowment of the old church was now established and that they would be looking for other members to work on this committee for ideas on how to approach this project. Anyone interested would be welcome.

March 13, 2006, inaugurated the first meeting of the Heritage Preservation Committee. The initial members were: Jerry Biltz, Joe Piazza and Debbie Scott who were appointed by Parish Council to this committee, Alice Biltz, Marge Conroy, Craig Edington, Barbara Kline, Patricia Knapp, Don and Joan Reisig, Shirley Riemenschneider, Helen White, and Robert Winkler.

The committee immediately went to work on issues of a leaking narthex roof, the question of removing the organ from the old church to the new, assembling an accurate timeline with dates and pictures of the priests and laity, and assessment of space and cabinet needs for display of historic items in an area that is planned to be available in the new church.

By the time the dedication of the new church arrived, the Heritage Preservation Committee had pictures of all the priests and others framed and hung on the back wall of the Narthex in the new church. From the above group of members came an amazing depth of memory about the leaders of St. Peter of the Fields. The parish is very fortunate to have had their insight and recollection and ability to find needed photographs. The wall of pictures in the new church is an invaluable history and is admired and studied constantly.

Don and Joan Reisig, Jerry Biltz, and Bob Winkler added technical and building skills to the committee. The men made much needed repairs to a leaking roof and rotting sills and doors. They also did painting, patching and more, all of which are ongoing projects. Bob Winkler Jr. and Bob Winkler Sr. repaired and stained the wooden crosses in the cemetery.

Barbara Kline did research on the Historical Register, and it was decided to wait before making an application. Joining the group were CeCe and Ray Knispel. Ray is knowledgeable on endowments and is an organized planner. His work on the committee addresses future planning and seeking of outside funding.

Meanwhile, Shirley Reimenschneider procured an Historic Church 1868 plaque. Craig Edington made up a handsome program for the dedication of the plaque. Father David Misbrenner conducted a brief but special blessing and the plaque can be seen by the front door of the church.

Rudy and Mary Tossenberg donated an organ to the historic church to replace the one that was moved to the new church. Larry and Helen White donated a beautiful, fully restored, upright piano to the old church for continuing, and hopefully growing, musical needs.

The Heritage Preservation Committee has cleaned and decorated the old church. Decorations go up as seasons change and plans are underway for uses of the building.

On May 17, 2008, Armed Forces Day, the committee hosted a celebration for the Portage County Bi-Centennial. There was a ceremony in the cemetery at which time three people buried there were honored. They were Magdalena Kissel, Adam Lansinger, and Reverend Walter J. Fowler.

In conclusion, the Historical Preservation Committee is comprised of a group of very dedicated members. They might be best described by Helen White's words that appeared in the *Record Courier*, October 3, 2004: "Those who treasure the legacy of the past . . . visit St. Peter of the Fields before it is too late. Bring your children, bring your families, and feel the awesome beauty and grace of a simple church. You don't need to travel to faraway lands to visit a monument to the religious history of the region. Remember this treasure in your heart, right here in Rootstown." We are trying to preserve it for the future.

Report #12
Report/Interview of Audrey Kissel Smith

Audrey Kissel Smith is one of the oldest members of St. Peter of the Fields. The information she provided paints an interesting picture of the early days of both St. Joseph's Church, Randolph, and St. Peter's, Rootstown.

Audrey Smith came to St. Peter's in 1940 at the age of 18. She married Charles Smith. Her father Joseph Kissel was baptized Catholic but was not a practicing Catholic, so Audrey was very happy when she became Catholic. She said that she sat on the front porch of the church rectory and received instructions from then Father Walter Fowler who told her not to worry about learning her religion. Father said that "It will come to you when your children go to Catechism." Audrey's Godparents were Dorothy Knapp Miller (wife of Herman Miller) and Philmore Smith (brother to her husband Charles).

Audrey was a member of the Holy Family Guild. St. Rita Ann was a branch of this guild and it met in various parish homes such as the Ambrose's, Kline's, Whittiker's and Turk's. It was a prayer and social type guild. The women made Christmas manger scenes and gave them to the Sunday school children. They also traded recipes with each other.

Audrey's great-grandmother Magdalena Kissel was the first person buried in St. Peter's Cemetery on March 16, 1867. Her great-grandfather John Kissel was a Civil War Veteran and is also buried at St. Peter's.

Audrey said she knew all the priests from Father Fowler to, and including, Father David Misbrenner (present pastor, 2010).

The following information from Audrey Kissel Smith was taken from the *Portrait and Biological Record of Portage and Summit Counties*, written in 1898.

Audrey said her grandfather John Kissel, a respected and prosperous farmer of Randolph township, Portage County, Ohio, and an ex-soldier of the Civil War, was born in Hesse Darmstadt, Germany, in March 1842, a son of Michael and Magdalena (Rice) Kissel, who were the parents of six children: Valentine and John, still living; Margaret who died November 30, 1866, the wife of Andrew Cook; Lizzie, wife of a Mr. Donnes, died in Illinois in 1878; Kate was the wife of Nicholas Sams and is also deceased; one child died in infancy. The father of the family died on shipboard when coming to this country in 1853 with his family, and the mother died here March 16, 1869.

John Kissel was about ten years of age when he landed in America with his mother and her family, after 100 days crossing the Atlantic Ocean. They settled in Rootstown, Portage County, where the mother purchased a farm, which was diligently cultivated by her two sons, who were aided by hired help. In January of 1865, John enlisted in Company H, 184th Ohio Volunteer Infantry, in which he served nine months and was honorably discharged September 25, 1865. Returning to Rootstown, he worked on the farm for his mother until 1868. On January 7, 1868, he married Miss Barbara Goodyear, daughter of Peter Goodyear, who was born in Germany, but came to America as a young man. He settled in Randolph Township, where he engaged in farming and married a Miss Bussel, who bore him five children, of whom three— John, George, and Barbara— are still living; Adam died in July 1897, aged 66 years, and Lizzie died in 1864. Both parents are now deceased, dying in the faith of the Church of Rome. The marriage of John Kissel and Miss Barbara Goodyear has been blessed with eleven children: Elizabeth, born July 17, 1869, was the wife of Burt Watters; Barbara, born February 14, 1871, was the wife of Martin Miller; George, born June 6, 1873; Kate, born July 28, 1875, was married to Jacob Luli; Mary, born June 2, 1877, was married to John Bentz; Lewis, born March 15, 1879; Adam, born February 12, 1881; Joseph, born January 10, 1883; Seth, born September 10, 1885; Clara, born October 29, 1888, was married to Lewis Huth on April 16, 1907; and Nina, born May 13, 1893.

In the spring of 1875, Mr. Kissel bought his present farm in Randolph Township, on which he settled in March of the same year, and in addition to general farming, has operated a threshing machine for the past nine years. He is a most excellent farmer, as everything around him fully attests, his fields being well drained, his fences always in good order, and his dwelling and farm structures being very neat and tasteful in appearance. Mr. Kissel has served as township supervisor one term. He and his family are members of St. Joseph's Catholic Church, to the support of which they contribute freely and liberally They are held in high esteem by all the members of the community in which they live.

Report #13
List of members of miscellaneous guilds at St. Peter's

12-January 1960 Newly Formed Guilds for St. Peter of the Fields.

Guild #1 St. Ann
Officers: Mesdames:
Mrs. H. Whittaker
Mrs. Roy H. Kline
Mrs. G. Moore Jr.
Mrs. John K. Kline
Members:
Mrs. P. Baber
Mrs. S. Kline
Mrs. Wm G. Kline
Mrs. W. Pletzer
Mrs. G. Turck
Mrs. C. Smith
Mrs. K. Smith
Mrs. P. Smith
Mrs. H. Carroll
Mrs. P. Teets
Miss Linda Kline

Guild #2 St. Catherine
Officers: Mesdames:
Mrs. R. Glass
Mrs. J. Miley
Mrs. C. Miley
Mrs. J. Rice
Members:
Mrs. J. Adam
Mrs. Mike Bildershein
Mrs. E. Kerr
Mrs. Russell Kline
Mrs. D. Knapp
Mrs. Ollie Knapp
Mrs. J. Robards
Mrs. M. Salandre
Mrs. A. Schwartz
Mrs. W. Wolford
Mrs. R. Bradley
Mrs. C. Bello
Mrs. H. Gamble
Mrs. P. Gieb
Miss Mary J. Knapp
Miss Rosemary Knapp
Miss Phylis Bradley

Guild #3 St. Martha:
Officers: Mesdames:
Mrs. J. Rodenbucher
Mrs. J. Winkler
Mrs. T. Magos Jr.
Mrs. R. Lamm
Members:
Mrs. J. Angebrandt
Mrs. K. Kline
Mrs. J. Leeway

#3 Contd.
Mrs. T. Magos Sr.
Mrs. A. Pizzute
Mrs. C. Rankin
Mrs. B. Streets
Miss C. Angebrandt
Miss Mary Winkler
Miss Marge Winkler

Guild #4 St. Mary
Officers: Mesdames:
Mrs. L. Biltz
Mrs. R. Knapp
Mrs. G. Rennie
Mrs. R. Kaltenbach
Members:
Mrs. V. Black
Mrs. W. Kenward
Mrs. G. Kline
Mrs. Wm J. Kline
Mrs. R. Mullaly
Mrs. G. Miller
Mrs. F. Polumbo
Mrs. P. Polumbo
Mrs. E. Riemenschneider
Mrs. D. Woolf
Mrs. R.W. Kline
Mrs. Robt. Kline
Mrs. B. Whitted
Miss Eloise Biltz

Guild #5 St. Odila
Officers: Mesdames:
Mrs. A. Gungle
Mrs. D. Goodhart
Mrs. P. Pritchard
Mrs. J. Sanders
Members:
Mrs. J. Branecky
Mrs. C. Conley
Mrs. Wm Conley
Mrs. O. Fulst
Mrs. C. Greenshield
Mr.s Geo Luli Jr.
Mrs. Waldo Sober Sr
Mr.s A. Swaney
Mrs. B. Szemplenski
Mrs. J. Bosko
Miss Evelyn Lynch

Guild #6 St. Rita
Officers: Mesdames:
Mrs. G. Luli Sr.

#6 Contd.
Mrs. C. Backalowski
Mrs. D. Franze
Mrs. W. Bockoven
Members:
Mrs. D. Armbruster
Mrs. L. Bisson
Mrs. J. Duffy
Mrs. J. Grant
Mrs. J. Knapp
Mrs. W. Luli
Miss G. Paulus
Mrs. S. Serva Sr.
Mrs. S. Ambrose
Mrs. S. Serva Jr.
Mrs. J. Serva.

Guild #7 St. Teresa
Officers: Mesdames:
Mrs. R. May Kline
Mrs. R. Strickling
Mrs. C. Brown
Mrs. G. Esposito
Members:

Mrs. W. Anthony
Mrs. A. Calabria
Mrs. J. Calabria
Mrs. J. Francis
Mrs. S. Francis
Mrs. A. Galzerano
Mrs. J. Kropac Jr.
Helen Mosher
Mrs. V. Nardo
Mrs. J. Nevitt
Mrs. B. Nowogrocki
Mrs. J. Krppac Sr.
Mrs. R. Sheaffer
Mrs. J. Slimak
Mrs. S. Bomarito
Mrs. M. Esposito
Mrs. S. Knapp
Mrs. E. Schuster
Mrs. R. Albright
Miss Carol Kline
Miss Rosemarie Anthon
Miss P. Strickling

The Alter & Rosary Society & Family Guild will continue as usual. The Guilds will help furnish the new kitchen.

159

Report #14
It Is Finished

Introduction
Christ Speaks
These fourteen steps that you are now about to walk, you do not take alone.
I walk with you. Though you are you, and I am I, yet we are truly one–one in Christ. And therefore my way of the cross two thousand years ago and your "way" now are also one. But note this difference. My life was incomplete until I crowned it by my death. Your fourteen steps will only be complete when you have crowned them by your life.

I: Jesus Is Condemned
Leader: We adore you, oh, Christ, and we praise you.
All: Because by your Holy Cross you have redeemed the world.
Pilate Speaks
All: My Jesus, Lord, obedience cost you your life. For me it cost an act of will—no more—and yet how hard it is for me to bend. Remove the blinders from my eyes that I may see that it is you whom I obey in all who govern me. Lord, it is you.
Leader: Lord Jesus crucified.
All: Have mercy on us.

II: Jesus Takes his Cross
Leader: We adore you, oh, Christ, and we praise you.
All: Because by your Holy Cross, you have redeemed the world.
Jesus Speaks
All: My Jesus, Lord, I take my daily cross. I welcome the monotony that often marks my day, discomforts of all kinds, the summer's heat, the winter's cold, my disappointments, tensions, setbacks, cares. Remind me often that in carrying my cross, I carry yours with you. And although I bear only a sliver of your cross, you carry all of mine, except a sliver, in return.
Leader: Lord Jesus crucified.
All: Have mercy on us.

III: Jesus Falls
Leader: We adore you, oh, Christ, and we praise you.
All: Because by your Holy Cross you have redeemed the world.
Jesus Speaks
All: Lord Jesus, how can I refuse? I willingly accept my weaknesses, my irritations and my moods, my headaches and fatigue, all the defects of body, mind and soul. Because they are your will for me, these "handicaps" of my humanity, I gladly suffer them. Make me content with all my discontents, but give me strength to struggle after you.
Leader: Lord Jesus crucified.
All: Have mercy on us.

IV: Jesus Meets His Mother
Leader: We adore you, oh, Christ, and we praise you.
All: Because by your Holy Cross you have redeemed the world.

Mary Speaks

My Jesus, Lord, I know what you are telling me. To watch the pain of those we love is harder then to bear our own. To carry my cross after you, I, too, must stand and watch the sufferings of my dear ones—the heartaches, sickness and grief of those I love. And I must let them watch mine too. I do believe—for those who love you all things together unto good.

Leader: Lord Jesus crucified.

All: Have mercy on us.

V: Simon Helps Jesus

Leader: We adore you, oh, Christ, and we praise you.

All: Because by your Holy Cross you have redeemed the world.

Simon Speaks

All: Lord, make me realize that every time I wipe a dish, pick up an object off the floor, assist a child in some small task, or give another preference in traffic or at the store, each time I feed the hungry, clothe the naked, teach the ignorant, or lend my hand in any way—it matters not to whom—my name is Simon. And the kindness I extend to them I really give to you.

Leader: Lord Jesus crucified.

All: Have mercy on us.

VI: Veronica Helps Jesus

Leader: We adore you, oh, Christ, and we praise you.

All: Because by your Holy Cross you have redeemed the world.

Veronica Speaks

All: Lord, what you ask is hard. It calls for courage and self-sacrifice, and I am weak. Please, give me strength. Don't let me run away because of fear. Lord, live in me and act in me and love in me. And not let me alone—in all of us—so that we may reveal no more your bloody but glorious face on earth.

Leader: Lord Jesus crucified.

All: Have mercy on us.

VII: Jesus Falls Again

Leader: We adore you, oh, Christ, and we praise you.

All: Because by your Holy Cross you have redeemed the world.

Jesus Speaks

All: Give me your courage, Lord. When failure presses heavily on me and I am desolate, stretch out your hand to lift me up. I know I must not cease, but preserve in doing good. But help me, Lord. Alone there is nothing I can do. With you, I can do anything you ask. I will.

Leader: Lord Jesus crucified.

All: Have mercy on us.

VIII: Jesus Consoles the Women

Leader: We adore you, oh, Christ, and we praise you.

All: Because by your Holy Cross you have redeemed the world.

The Women Speak

All: My Jesus, your compassion in your passion is beyond compare. Lord, teach me, help me learn. When I would snap at those who hurt me with their ridicule, those who misunderstand, or hinder me with some misguided helpfulness, those who intrude upon my privacy—then help me curb my tongue. May gentleness become my cloak. Lord, make me kind like you.

Leader: Lord Jesus crucified.

All: Have mercy on us.

IX: The Third Fall

Leader: We adore you, oh, Christ, and we praise you.

All: Because by your Holy Cross you have redeemed the world.

Jesus Speaks

All: My Lord, I see you take a moment's rest then rise and stagger on. So I can do because my will is mine. When all my strength is gone and guilt and self-reproach press me to earth and seem to hold me fast, protect me from the sin of Judas—save me from despair! Lord, never let me feel that any sin of mine is greater than your love. No matter what my past has been I can begin anew.

Leader: Lord Jesus crucified.

All: Have mercy on us.

X: Jesus Is Stripped

Leader: We adore you, oh, Christ, and we praise you.

All: Because by your Holy Cross you have redeemed the world.

The Soldier Speaks

All: My Lord, I offer you my all—whatever I possess, and more, my self. Detach me from the craving for prestige, position, wealth. Root out of me all trace of envy of my neighbor who has more than I. Release me from the vice of pride, my longing to exalt myself, and lead me to the lowest place. May I be poor in spirit, Lord, so that I can be rich in you.

Leader: Lord Jesus crucified.

All: Have mercy on us.

XI: Jesus Is Crucified

Leader: We adore you, oh, Christ, and we praise you.

All: Because by your Holy Cross you have redeemed the world.

A Boy Speaks

All: My God, I look at you and think: Is my soul worth this much? What can I give you in return? I here and now accept for all my life what ever sickness, torment, agony may come. To every cross I touch my lips. O blessed cross that lets me be—with you—a co-redeemer of humanity.

Leader: Lord Jesus crucified.

All: Have mercy on us.

XII: Jesus Dies

Leader: We adore you, oh, Christ, and we praise you.

All: Because by your Holy Cross you have redeemed the world.

Jesus Speaks

All: My Jesus, God, what can I say or do? I offer you **my** death with all its sins, accepting now the time and kind of death in store for me. Not by a single instant would I lengthen my life's span. I offer you my death for my own sins and for those of all humanity. My God! My God! Forsake us not. We know not what we do.

Leader: Lord Jesus crucified.

All: Have mercy on us.

XIII: Jesus Is Taken Down

Leader: We adore you, oh, Christ, and we praise you.

All: Because by your Holy Cross you have redeemed the world.

Mary Speaks

All: I beg you, Lord, help me accept the partings that must come—from friends who go away, my children leaving home, and most of all, my dear ones when you shall call them to yourself. Then, give me grace to say: "As it has pleased you, Lord, to take them home, I bow to you most holy will, and if by just one word I might restore their lives against your will, I would not speak." Grant them eternal joy.

Leader: Lord Jesus crucified.

All: Have mercy on us.

XIV: Jesus Is Buried

Leader: We adore you, oh, Christ, and we praise you.

All: Because by your Holy Cross you have redeemed the world.

Joseph Speaks

All: My Jesus, Lord, you know my spirit is as willing as my flesh is weak. The teaching you could not impart, the sufferings you could not bear, the works of love you could not do in your short life on earth, let me impart, and bear, and do, through you. But I am nothing, Lord. Help me!

Leader: Lord Jesus crucified.

All: Have mercy on us.

Conclusion

I told you at the start, my other self, my life was not complete until I crowned it by my death. Your "way" is not complete unless you crown it by your life. Accept each moment as it comes to you, with faith and trust that all that happens has my mark on it. A simple *Fiat*, this is all it takes; a breathing in your heart, "I will it, Lord." So seek me not in far-off places. I am close at hand. Your workbench, office, kitchen, these altars where you offer love. And I am with you there. Go now! Take up your cross and with your life complete your way. Amen.

Report #15
The life of Saint John Nepomucene Neumann
1811-1860

St. John Neumann was a true Bishop & Shepherd who followed in the footsteps of his Master Jesus Christ. He believed that he was bishop for only one reason and that reason was to save souls. St. John was the Archbishop of Philadelphia for only eight short years, but in that time he built eighty churches and forty schools. So concerned was he for the salvation of souls that he did this in spite of his overwhelming diocesan debt. After all, he was ordained Bishop to shepherd and save souls. His idea of stewardship was spiritual not material.

Under his reign vocations to the priesthood increased. He established a congregation of teaching Sisters and he is credited as the founder of the Catholic Parochial School System in the United States, which, before 1960, was the largest private school system in the world. He wrote a catechism for children and adults as well as Bible History for adults.

In his great love for Jesus in the blessed Sacrament, St. John Neumann established the practice of the Diocesan-wide Forty Hours Devotions in Philadelphia which eventually spread throughout the United States. He visited all his parishes and priests on a regular schedule to encourage the Faith and build up his diocese. He lived simply and prayerfully for the Church, devoted to the Blessed Sacrament and the Virgin Mary. His favorite pious invocation was, "Lord, there is nothing going to happen to me today that You and I together cannot handle." The motto he chose as Bishop was "Passion of Christ Strengthen Me."

Even though St. John Neumann lived in the early 1800s, his theology of the building up of the Church was what it always has been and always will be. Reading from the *Catechism of the Catholic Church* we find the motivation of St. John Neumann for spreading the Gospel and saving souls as relevant today as it was in his day:

> 849 *The missionary mandate.* "Having been Divinely sent to the nations that she might be 'the universal sacrament of salvation,' the Church, in obedience to the command of her Founder and because it is demanded by her own essential university, strives to preach the Gospel to all men." (Ad gentes 1) "Go therefore and make disciples of all nations, baptizing them in the name of the Father and of the Son and of the Holy Spirit, teaching them to observe all that I have commanded you; and Lo, I am with you always, until the close of the age." (St. Matthew 28:19-20)

St. John Neumann is perhaps the best example and patron we in the United States can have today. He is the first male saint canonized in our country. He worked tirelessly for the building up of the Church. He saw the spiritual needs of his Diocese as the focus of his life and work and the sole reason for his vocation. He understood and believed that if we seek first the kingdom of God (St. Matthew 6:33) everything else will follow, everything else will be provided. He had his priorities and they were the priorities of Jesus Christ. Can you and I have any other?

St. John Neumann had a very intense devotion to St. Philomena and her statue can be found on the east wall of the new church next to his photo.

Report #16
Interview of Aunts Cathryn and Julia

My aunt Cathryn Winkler Miller, born in 1910, and my aunt Julia Winkler Fitt, born in 1914, said they learned to do the Charleston from Mary and Grace Kline, daughters of Henry C. Kline. This was a popular dance in the U.S. in the 1900s.

Aunt Julia said that as a young girl she remembered waiting all week long just to go to the church social where she got an ice cream cone for five cents. My aunts both said they remembered the wooden side benches around the church basement. This was the seating arrangement in the 1930s.

Julia also related that her mother Margaret Knapp Winkler bought a Model T Ford from Johnny Knapp. Julia taught herself to drive this car at age fourteen by driving it around the large east field of their farm where this author lives today. She said that she drove her mother to church, and her mom would sit on the edge of the seat and pray all the way there because she was so afraid of the car.

Julia played left guard on Rootstown's girls' basketball team and they won every game until the tournaments at Kent State University, which was called Kent Normal School at that time, where they lost their first game. Julia said that they were scared to death of the big college atmosphere. The principal at this time was Ward Davis whose name appears on the present high school building at Rootstown. Helen Smith, who presently lives in Florida, was the team coach. Members of the team were Dorothy Garren, Leeta Ely, Louise and Hilda Louwellin, and Edith Seeman. As we read in Chapter V, Julia and Cathryn were church organists and played at a very early age while at St. Peter's.

Aunt Julia and Aunt Cathryn's father, John Winkler, born in Bierstadt, Germany, 1865, came to the United States at age 17 and was one of the early parishioners of St. Peter's. He had three sisters: Eva, Nancy, and Anna. Nancy's son Franz Kock was sent for and came to the United States. The interview of my aunts Julia and Cathryn provided much useful and appropriate information on the early social programs at St. Peter's and are placed in this chapter for that reason.

Acknowledgments

This book would not have the flavor it provides if it were not for those listed here. The author is greatly appreciative of the interest and time given by these persons whose information was attained by interview or from personal collection:

Irene Lang May
Isabelle Biltz Moore
Eloise Biltz Sweet
Alma Biltz Winkler
Shirley Biltz Riemenschneider
William and Florence Kline
Henry and Barb Kline
Julia Winkler Fitt
Cathryn Winkler Miller
Lawrence Winkler
Bill Winkler
John L. Winkler (author's father)
James H. Winkler
Raymond Luli
Mary Winkler Wise
Dolores Herman
Audrey Kissel Smith
Helen Ambrose Gless
Chuck Miley
Sister Regina
Father Terrance Hazel
Father John Sargent
Jack Guzi
Stanley and Caroline Ambrose
Paul Knapp
Betty Biltz King
J. Kenneth and Rose Kline
Edith Englehart
Diocese of Cleveland Archives
 Chris Krossel
Catholic University of Washington D.C
 Jane Stoeffler
Kent State University Archives
Youngstown Diocese - Nancy Yuhasz
Joanne Kranz Jordan
Rose Duffy
Helen Winkler Parry

Deacon Tom and Sherrie Shay
Dorthy Luli
Helen White
Ester Koval
Jim Ward
Ted Ambacher
Kathy Ehasz
Mary Postlethwait
Marge and William Conroy
John Wischt
Mike Wischt
Special Recognition goes to:
Jane Paulus Bedard
Rita Paulus Kotkowski
Dave and Connie Moulton
Joe Grahm
Paul and Judy Kriegar
Bob Lux
Deborah Tatro
William Kelley
Gerald and Alice Biltz
Martin Knipp
Richard and Judy Hendershot
Ann Brown
Barney Trares
Larry Mudd
Vernon Clapp
Lee Jenior
Mitch Jenior
Jeff Knapp
Steve Francis
Dave Moulton
Mary Stricklin
Jim Nestich
Marie Rice
Joan Rice
Larry Bresky

Rebecca Winkler (author's granddaughter for typing the entire manuscript)

Monica Winkler Myers (author's daughter for photo and format editor)

Janet Stadulis (for being the manuscript editor)

Helen White (member of St. Peter's Heritage Preservation Committee) for her encouragement and continued support for this project.

*I apologize to anyone who assisted with this book but whose name was inadvertently omitted from these acknowledgements.

References

Rootstown Sesquicentennial. July 4-6, 1952

Edward Dominic Fenwick Papers 1803-1832

Pioneer History (1802-1865) by Walter Johnson Dickenson

St. Joseph Church 1831-2006 175th Anniversary Book

Souvenir Booklet. July 19, 1959. St. Peter of the Fields 90th Anniversary Celebration Rootstown, Ohio 1869-1959

St. Peter of the Fields, Rootstown, Ohio 125th Anniversary Celebration 1868-1993

Celebration of the Dedication Mass, St. Peter of the Fields Catholic Church 2006

St. Peter of the Fields Church Directory 1991

St. Peter of the Fields Centennial Year 1868-1968

St. Peter of the Fields Catholic Church Dedication 2006

Jubilee 2000 Booklet, St. Peter of the Fields

A Portrait and Biographic Record of Portage & Summit Counties, Ohio. 1898

The Amazing Father Lindesmith by Monsignor James R. Kolp, 2004

Historical Sketch and Reminiscences of St. Joseph's Church, Randolph, Ohio 1931

Diocese of Cleveland, *Prehistory to Founding in 1847,* Rev. W.A. Jurgens

March of the Eucharist by the Catholic Diocese of Cleveland, Archives

Kent State University Archives, papers from St. Peter of the Fields

Catholic University of America, Washington D.C. Archives

Announcement Book. January 1900. St. Peter's Church, Rootstown, Ohio, John J. Boyle

Record Courier, newspaper. Ravenna, Ohio

Catholic Diocese of Youngstown, Archives

Our Lady of the Elms Convent & School, Sister Rebecca Beltz

Combination Atlas Map of Portage County 1874

St. Peter's Weekly *Gleaning.* June 30, 1945

Portage Heritage by James B. Holm

A History of Catholicity in Northern Ohio and in the Diocese of Cleveland, by Michael W. Carr 1903

Catholic Diocese of Grand Rapids Michigan, Archives Curator, Fr. Phil Sliwinski

ABOUT THE AUTHOR -Written by a Fellow Parishioner

Perhaps it was destiny that Robert F. Winkler found himself drawn to the project of writing "Journey to St. Peter of the Fields." He possesses special qualities that created the desire and ability to write about this small Catholic parish in rural Ohio. As part of the combined factors, the Winkler family played an important part. As early settlers, the Winklers were instrumental in the initial purchase of the land where the church was built. In the historic cemetery behind the church, stone markers with the Winkler name stand as testaments of family ties. Many of his ancestors lived their lives through St. Peters of the Fields, as did Robert's parents, John L. and Marie Winkler, who brought him up in the Faith. In 1958 Robert married Dolores Kelley and they raised their children, Judy, Monica, Robert and John in this historic church.

Career wise, Robert drew on a sense of duty to country and joined the Army Airborne and served three years in the 82nd Airborne Division at Fort Bragg, North Carolina. He is proudly patriotic and is often seen in uniform assisting the St. Peter of the Fields Catholic War Veterans, whose formation at St. Peter's, he initiated.

He served as a State Highway Patrolman for the State of Ohio, at the Castalia, Massillon, and Ravenna Posts. Additionally he served at the Kent State University Police Department as Deputy Chief of Police and as a Lieutenant in the Portage County Sheriff's Department. He ended his career as Court Administrator at the Portage County Juvenile Court and Detention Center.

With deeply held religious beliefs, Robert has fine moral character and principals. He possesses strong feelings for doing what is right and is honest, loyal, and dedicated. These traits manifest themselves in a person willing to do good for all. Using his personal talents and an extraordinary amount of time and effort he has carefully written this Historic Sketch of his church. It has taken ten years to assemble information, pictures and historical data. The contents of the book, covers a span of over two hundred years to the present. Included within these pages is documentation from Rootstown and Randolph Townships. He has secured personal records of several of the early priests; and he has done archival study and interviews of present and former parishioners from both St. Peter of the Fields and St. Joseph's Parish in Randolph, Ohio.

Encouraged by parishioners, family and friends, Robert has captured events and people within the parish and preserved irreplaceable memories from days gone by, for future members and for those who enjoy history. "Job Well Done!"